Hooked On

Literature

Hooked On
Literature

How to Make Literature Exciting for Kids

Jamie Whitfield

Library of Congress Cataloging-in-Publication Data
Whitfield, Jamie, 1952-
    Hooked on literature : how to make literature exciting for kids / Jamie
Whitfield.
        p. cm.
    Includes bibliographical references.
    ISBN 1-59363-161-8 (pbk.)
    1. Literature--Study and teaching (Elementary) 2. Activity programs in
education. I. Title.
    LB1575.W524 2005
    372.64--dc22   2005018384

PRUFROCK PRESS INC.
P.O. Box 8813
Waco, TX 76714-8813
(800) 998-2208
http://www.prufrock.com

For Aunt Lillian who, long after leaving the classroom,
continues teaching life's valuable lessons.

Precious Words

He ate and drank the precious words,
His spirit grew robust;
He knew no more that he was poor,
Nor that his frame was dust.
He danced along the dingy days,
And this bequest of wings
Was but a book. What liberty
A loosened spirit brings!

—Emily Dickinson

Table of Contents

Preface

"What's the last thing you've read?"

It seemed like an easy question for a room of English teachers. But there was a long silence. There were the expected mumbles about having no time to read anything but student papers and then a second of silence. A cautious voice or two described reading new textbooks to try to keep ahead of students, and then more silence.

There were a few who dutifully noted having "just finished" something written by an author whose name was obviously chosen to impress the rest of the room. Then there was a very long silence and averted eyes.

It is very true that the business of teaching leaves little time for leisurely reading. Many of us save our "fun" reading for the summer. So do many students, and that's a shame.

What is the last thing you've read? Why did you read it? Was it an outstanding piece of *literature* that totally absorbed you, taking you to another place and time, or was it the morning newspaper, gobbled as quickly as your breakfast? Perhaps it was the latest curriculum guidelines or the next chapter in your text? A billboard? The want ads?

Recently, I began my day reading the newspaper, quickly scanning headlines, stopping here and there when a particular lead caught my attention. Except for the few words on an occasional billboard, I did no further reading until I arrived at school and picked up what was in my teacher's box, reading the adjusted schedule for assembly, the request for a parent conference, the results of a disciplinary notice, and the daily bulletin. I began reading a memo from the principal concerning deadlines for report card information, but, realizing it was a recycling of last year's memo, I stopped and filed it.

Throughout the day, I read snatches of student papers and a note sent from another teacher asking me to cover a class. During my planning period, the latest district memo concerning the changes in the statewide test and four student papers set for conferences the next day took up my time. I also visited my box twice more, reading, filing, and throwing away as needed (mostly throwing away).

Once home, I read the remaining three student papers, glanced through two magazines and fell asleep after two chapters in a highly recommended novel I am desperately trying to finish.

You can see that each type of reading came from a different need, ranging from the necessity of staying current with the school's newest requirements to the enjoyment of vicariously escaping the realities of teaching—each need requiring a varying amount of attention to detail, with a few needing no attention at all. You can also easily see I love to read. Many students do not. The following lessons were designed for those students—and for the teachers whose classrooms they fill.

I've tried to make the lessons accessible to teachers, regardless of the age or level of students they encounter, by having strands of generic themes (i.e., love, values, justice) run through each of the chapter sections. I have also included suggested readings. At the end of the book, you will find examples of lessons based on particular readings and units that incorporate the activities found in the book.

Chapter One

Introduction

Reading is to the mind what exercise is to the body.
—Sir Richard Steele

Donald Murray (1989) feels those who hate reading "may be the majority of students, parents, teachers, and administrators in any school system." He believes those who hate reading do so because they fear reading, a fear that "comes from the school-indoctrinated notion that there is one correct meaning for every text" (p. 17).

Take time to listen the next time literature, or more likely a movie, is discussed in the teachers' lounge. The strengths or weaknesses of plot, the motivation of character, the development of theme—all are part of what helps form opinions about stories, whether they are found in literature or on film. Chances are some of these topics will emerge during the conversation in the lounge, and there will be differences in opinion.

Advocates of each opposing view will defend his or her own opinion. Maybe one side will point out something to convince the other to change, but probably the bell will ring before the discussion is over, with no agreement of right or wrong.

If this happens in our classrooms with students reading an assigned text, each debating relevant points from the text until the bell rings, the discussion is considered a success. Yet, it seldom happens in the classroom. Many students rarely read the assigned text; in fact, they often complain about having to read it at all.

Zillions magazine recently conducted a survey asking students to list their number one "gripe" about school. The number one gripe, receiving 28% of the votes, was *boredom*, followed by *poor grades* at 13%.

Students were also asked to list the one thing they liked best about school. *Interesting classes* (32%) beat out *being with friends* (23%).

Many of us claim that the only reason students come to class is to be with their friends, and once there, their only motivation is the carrot-stick game called grading. Yet, when responding to a magazine catering to their peers, students were most concerned with what occurs during classtime. They didn't want to be bored; they wanted to be interested in what was happening during that particular block of time. It is a block of time controlled by teachers.

When teachers are able to move from center stage and allow students to become actively engaged in their work, students are virtually forced to be responsible for whether their work is interesting or boring. However, many teachers are reluctant to move out of the spotlight for fear that giving up total control of a classroom means giving up a measure of successful student performance. Yet, according to George H. Wood's (1993) *Schools That Work: America's Most Innovative Public Education Programs*, successful schools are those where "learning is not a spectator sport."

I am not a good spectator at a football game. In fact, I have some friends who, because they love the game, refuse to attend with me. I watch everyone in the stands, I try each new cheer, I do everything but watch the game. I'm simply not interested. Yet, through the years, I have attended enough games to know the basics of it. For example, I know that when a referee throws both arms straight into the air it means there was a touchdown, but I have to glance at the scoreboard to know who made it.

A lot of my friends are completely enthralled by football. They know every nuance of the game and are as interested in what's happening on the field as if they were out there playing themselves. Some of them are still patient enough to sit with me and, on the rare occasion that I want to know what's going on, will answer even the most mundane questions for me, knowing that while I enjoy being with them, I'm really not interested in football.

I think many students feel the same way about the subject I teach. They've learned enough to go from grade to grade, with the help of patient friends and teachers, and they know what's going on in the room. But they're really not interested in reading. According to the *Zillions* survey, they don't want to be bored. They want to be in interesting classes with people they consider friends, and they hope to make good grades.

It would seem logical then that a teacher would try to develop lessons that allow students to interact with both the literature and each other—lessons that allow the students to connect the literature to their own lives. This is not a new idea.

As early as the 17th century, John Amos Comenius believed learning should not only be enjoyable, but also tied to the real lives of students. This idea has been echoed by such paragons of education as Jean-Jacques Rousseau, who observed acquiring knowledge from the vantage point of romantic realism; John Dewey, who viewed learning as a practical experience; and Lev Vygotsky, who looked at education through the lens of social behavior. However, when Eliot Wigginton approached the curricular requirements of an English classroom by having students publish their own magazine, *Foxfire*, it was seen as a new, non-traditional approach. When Johnson and Johnson advocate collaborative learning techniques, many teachers take a won't-work-with-my-students attitude.

Yet, in order to function well in a democratic society, students need the attitudes and values that can be learned in well-prepared collaborative lessons and through the vicarious experiences they encounter when they actively engage in reading a wide range of literature. If, as Wigginton notes in *Core Practices* (for more information see *Hands On*, Foxfire Fund, Rabin Gap, GA 30568), the attitudes and values teachers model toward their students, the subject area, and the class work are important, why do we so often feel compelled to offer little more than lists of study questions followed by multiple-choice tests?

Our time is limited. Our resources are limited.

But, until we allow "extensive time to read, an effective choice in choosing their books, and change our approach to classroom grouping," Donald Graves believes, "[we] will find few lifelong readers and writers." While agreeing with Graves' statement, I hasten to add that I have taught in systems with prescribed reading lists, which not only set the sequence of the readings, but also allot the amount of time given to each reading to ensure all students have access to each selection, no matter how briefly.

Copies were limited, budget was tight, and it was believed that each selection had literary merit. Despite the concern many educators voice about students who skim the surface of literature and think they can acquire any necessary, in-depth understanding from a movie or Cliff's Notes, we were required to channel-surf our way through wonderful classics.

This channel-surfing approach to reading was not based on research or successful practice or even just someone's theory—the sole justification of this approach was economic. It eliminated the luxury of quiet reading days I had experienced in another school system where we were allowed to pick and choose our reading selections according to the needs and interests of our students. With the prescribed list and time table, I tried to create enough interest in the reading selection to motivate students to spend time outside the classroom.

So, I counted on their need for social interaction. I appealed to their creative tendencies. I hoped their natural curiosity would kick in. I devised evaluation methods that did not rely solely on essay or multiple-choice. I am including the most successful lessons in this book.

Chapter Two

Conversations, Discussions, and Debates

There is only one good, knowledge, and one evil, ignorance.
—Socrates

Talking occurs naturally in classrooms, and with a little planning it can be the stimulus for student reading. Letting students know that reading will lead to their being able to talk, *really* talk, is the key. The problem is the difference between what teachers mean by *really* talk (you listen while I talk or you can talk as long as you say what I want you to say) and what students mean (I will have a chance to voice my own opinion).

Too often, teachers will finish a lesson thinking there was a wonderful classwide discussion when, in fact, there was a wonderful discussion between two people—the teacher was one person and all the others in the class functioned as the other person.

I doubted this at first, until I noted that when my classes were having "discussions" I was the focal point. In other words, I would make a statement. A student, when acknowledged by me, would respond to the statement. I would respond to that student and either acknowledge another student or move to another topic. I even controlled the choice of discussion topics.

Contrast this to the way most large groups of people converse.

- Sometimes, more than one person speaks at once, causing the conversation group to momentarily break into small sub-groups.

- There are often "voice overs" where one person begins to add to the conversation just before another is finished.

- Very seldom is anyone chastised for only listening.

- People tend to listen to the person who appears to have the most information or is the most entertaining.

I'm not advocating that classrooms become the chaotic noise dens found in the hallways during class breaks. I am also not saying there is never a time or reason for a lecture. I'm just cautioning you to be aware that the types of conversations, discussions, and debates that occur in the "real world," for which we are supposed to be preparing students, are seldom offered to students within the classroom.

The lessons in this book were designed to offer students the opportunity to practice such experiences. Although I have used particular works of literature as examples in the lessons, you could easily plug other works into each lesson. To be successful, look for unresolved conflict (which all literature contains), for a contradiction, and for a point of contention.

The work should have enough evidence to support more than one side; otherwise your students will feel the practice is as futile as discussing the shape of the Earth or debating the cheese content of the moon. Remember, you are trying to prepare students to state opinions articulately, based on evidence (not emotion or conjecture)—a valuable skill in the "real world."

Unless otherwise noted, worksheets listed under each lesson's **Materials Needed** can be found at the end of that lesson. Materials not found in the book are marked with an asterisk.

Lesson One

Literature:	"Thank You, Ma'am" by Langston Hughes
Strand:	Justice
Activity:	Discussion based on letters and postcards
Timeline:	2–3 days
Materials Needed:	Postcards Grading Rubric Discussion Tracker (found in Lesson Two)
Learning Objectives:	Students will (1) understand the various points of views of characters in the story; (2) predict outcomes based on evidence in the story; and (3) write letters or postcards.
Lesson Summary:	Students will read the short story and then take on the persona of each character projected into the future. One character writes to a second character, and the second character responds. The teacher functions as a post office, receiving and dispensing the letters and postcards, evaluating them based on pre-established criteria.

Background Information

The Literature:

The short story "Thank You, Ma'am" tells of a young boy named Roger who, wanting money for new shoes, decides to steal the pocket book of Mrs. Luella Bates Washington Jones, an old woman on the street. Mrs. Jones proves to be no easy mark for Roger as she fights back, puts him in a half nelson, and eventually takes him to her home. There, she has him clean up, gives him something to eat, and, finally, gives him the money he had tried to steal.

The piece is full of discussion material, such as stereotypes of criminals and the elderly as well as the idea of appropriate retribution for crime. Presenting this lesson near the beginning of the year is most helpful because it can easily lead to discussion about consequences of inappropriate classroom behavior, often leading students to develop their own Code of Honor.

The Activity:

If it is true that writing helps us clarify our thoughts, what better way to prepare for a discussion than to put thoughts to paper? Yet some students are crippled by fear of committing their thoughts to paper—afraid their ideas are "not good enough." Who wouldn't be a little apprehensive about writing their ideas on justice or punishment or rehabilitation of criminals and then being asked to discuss those ideas in front of a large group of people?

By allowing students to take on the personality of someone else (e.g., a character in a piece of literature), you are allowing them to voice their opinions in a decidedly nonthreatening way. They formulate, sometimes subconsciously, their ideas on such powerful topics within the framework of fiction. By projecting themselves into the lives and minds of characters, students try on opinions and attitudes about issues that will surround them as they leave school and face the real world. Writing from the point of view of a fictional character gives students a certain anonymity to explore their own opinions, and writing from the point of view of two seemingly opposing characters gives them enough space to try on more than one opinion. That's why I find the second postcard in this exercise an essential part of the lesson.

Lesson Outline:

1. Begin the lesson on restitution by asking: "If something were stolen and the thief were caught, what would be proper punishment?" Listen to comments, but (to avoid having students parrot what you've said) make no comment of your own.

2. After students have commented, introduce the idea behind the story—a young man has tried to steal from an elderly woman. Allow students time to read the story (perhaps overnight).

3. Discuss the story with the students. I usually begin by asking what they think happened to Roger as a result of his encounter with Mrs. Jones.

4. After the initial discussion, have each student take the position of Roger and Mrs. Jones. First, taking on the persona of Roger 20 years after the story, each student writes to Mrs. Jones describing Roger's present life and the impact his encounter with her has had on it. Tell students that you will collect their letters and then give them to other students who will respond as Mrs. Jones.

5. Collect letters and check them for the established grading criteria (see section on Evaluation) and then forward the letters to other students. I randomly choose who will receive each letter.

6. Each student takes on the persona of Mrs. Jones 20 years after the story and answers the letter he or she received from Roger. Mrs. Jones responds to what Roger has written and describes how she feels about their encounter.

7. Collect the letters again and give them back to the correct "Roger."

8. Allot time for additional class discussion about the exercise. I begin by asking students to share letters and responses and to discuss their ideas on appropriate retribution for Roger.

Evaluation:

This lesson, requiring each student to generate two letters and the teacher to produce a quick turn-around, can result in a mind-boggling grade feast for any teacher. I have never wanted to meticulously grade 200–250 pieces of writing in a span of a few days.

There are some ways to handle this lesson so that it produces manageable grading documents. First, I require students to use postcards, giving them the opportunity to use actual postcards of their own or use the ones I provide (some students personalize these with illustrations). The size of the postcard not only limits the volume of writing, it also forces students to focus on what they want to say.

Next, I tie my grading to one or two particular items, creating a rubric of no more than two or three items. Depending on the level of students, the rubric can deal with only the front of the postcard (forwarding and return addresses); the mechanics of the message (requiring a minimum number of sentences, for example, and then looking only at the end punctuation or requiring particular types of comma usage); portions of the content (citing evidence from the literature to support their predictions); or a combination of the above.

Before beginning the assignment, make sure that students are fully aware of the method and focus of the grading system for this exercise. I have found it useful to ask for student input when developing a grading rubric.

Sample Rubrics

Postcard

Item	Point Value	Points Earned	Total
Capitalization used correctly	33		
Abbreviations used correctly	33		
Commas used correctly	34		

Comments:

Postcard

Item	Point Value	Points Earned	Total
Forward/Return Address	33		
Punctuation	33		
Prediction/Evidence	34		

Comments:

Postcards

Dear

To:

23¢
USA

Dear

To:

23¢
USA

Lesson Two

Literature:	"All the Years of Her Life" by Morley Callaghan
Strand:	Justice
Activity:	Discussion
Time Line:	1–2 days
Materials Needed:	Evidence Organizer Discussion Tracker Law Proposal
Learning Objectives:	Students will (1) participate in small and large group discussion and (2) research evidence to use in a debate.
Lesson Summary:	After reading the story, students participate in both small and large group discussions centered on the topic of justice. Using reference materials, as well as the story, students will prepare for a classroom debate.

Background Information

The Literature:

The short story "All the Years of Her Life" covers the night a young man is caught stealing from the drug store where he works. After confronting him, the manager calls the boy's mother. Her demeanor once she reaches the drug store is both surprising and disquieting for the boy and his manager. Instead of calling the police, the manager allows the young man to go home with his mother. The story ends as the young man, silently observing his mother at home, has an awakening.

This piece is ripe with discussion material, with the most blatant topic centered on the theme of "unpunished" crime. I usually present this lesson in conjunction with "Thank You, Ma'am," as they deal with the same issues. Using the stories together allows students to gauge the ideas they formulated in one story against different characters and circumstances.

The Activity:

Tedious is the word that most accurately describes the classroom discussions I face at the beginning of each year. That is one of the reasons I incorporate this lesson into the curriculum as quickly as possible. It easily leads to students discussing their ideas on justice (and once I understand their ideas and they understand mine, class usually runs more smoothly), and it helps students understand what I mean by *discussion*.

Discussion Does Not Mean:	Discussion Means:
I talk. You listen and take notes.	Everyone's voice carries equal weight.
You only speak when I call on you.	Manners and social customs dictate when the next person speaks.
I decide what to talk about. No straying off topic.	Ideas may lead us to other topics.
Your opinion is valid, as long as it is my opinion.	A valid opinion is one based on facts.
You are speaking only to me, so don't make side comments to your neighbor.	The life of a conversation is fluid, moving from the whole group to small sub-groups and back.

I take several steps prior to and during this lesson to help students understand how serious I am about having *real* discussions in which each voice is valued. After a few classroom discussions, students are usually more than willing to participate in meaningful dialogue, so I drop the steps. However, I occasionally revive one or two of them as needed throughout the year—usually when the topic is one in which I am so interested that there is a danger of my using my status as a teacher to dominate the discussion.

1. **Arranging the Group**

   Most classrooms are arranged so that students see the face of the teacher at the front and the backs of each other's heads. This does not allow them to pick up on subtle, non-verbal clues such as eye movement and facial expressions, which alert members of a conversational group when a person is finishing a point or wants to make a statement. I explain this to the students and ask them to move desks or chairs into a circle so that everyone has a clear view of everyone else.

2. **Avoiding Power Plays**

   It is often easy to spot any member of a conversation group who has power or dominance over other members. Watch how teachers respond during a discussion at a faculty meeting. To give the appearance of listening, most turn their heads or eyes toward the speaker, who is usually an administrator, at the front of the room.

Eyes and heads turn toward any colleague who is acknowledged and given a turn to speak, but once that speaker is finished, all eyes and heads turn back toward the front of the room, waiting for the person in charge to designate the next speaker. Designation does not always mean calling someone's name; it can be as subtle as looking toward someone and giving a nod of the head, a cock of the eyebrow, or a smile, and the next person allowed to speak knows it is his or her turn.

I warn students of these power plays and alert them to avoid looking my way for recognition. It is a hard habit to break, and my best weapon is a Discussion Tracker. It forces me to keep my eyes cast down at the paper, allows students to develop the non-verbal behaviors necessary to participating in discussions, and makes them aware that I am not ignoring their opinions. Quite the contrary, I value their opinions highly enough to want to record them.

3. Beginning the Discussion

Once we are all in place and settled, I begin by stating the discussion topic. Once I have done that, I bow my head, poise my pen, and wait for students to begin the discussion. There is always an awkward moment while students look to each other for clues as to who should begin, but I have always had one or two students who rush in to fill the silence. And that's okay, as long as *I* don't rush in.

4. Handling Extended Silences

Despite the belief that allowing students free rein in discussions would result in chaos, most teachers are not prepared for the silences that occur. If those silences are the result of students digesting an interesting point that has just been made or if a speaker is trying to collect thoughts, I simply remain with eyes down and pen ready. These types of silences sometimes occur and to rush in with a comment merely to break the silence would defeat the idea of having discussions.

However, the silence could be the result of students having said all they really have to say about the topic and to force them to continue just to end the silence would also defeat the purpose of having discussions. It might be wise to move on to a related discussion.

Lesson Outline:

1. Begin this lesson by asking: "If you stole something and were caught, what would happen to you?" At the end of the discussion, introduce the idea behind the story—a young man has been caught stealing from his employer. Ask for opinions on what should happen to the young man.

2. Before students begin reading, tell them they will be participating in discussions about the story and will need to track evidence in the story concerning the actions

of each character. To do this, I provide each student with an Evidence Organizer and the instructions to write down *anything* that strikes them about a character's actions.

3. Once they have finished reading, have students move so they can participate in a classwide discussion (see Activity Section). Tell the class that you will be using the Discussion Tracker to record their ideas and then ask them to discuss, using evidence from the story, the following question: **If it is true that each action causes a reaction, what could each of the characters have done differently to prevent the theft from occurring?** (For example, the manager could have talked with the boy when he first suspected he was stealing; the mother could have taken a firmer stand in disciplining the boy.)

4. Track the class discussion for the allotted time. I allow about 20 minutes, but I'm very flexible with that time, prepared to run longer if needed and also to move to the next portion of the lesson if they truly run out of anything to say. Then, ask the students if they know of any existing laws that would have prevented any of the characters' actions. The most obvious replies will address the laws against shoplifting, but try to move students to focus on the manager and the mother also. They will soon be informally debating whether or not there should be laws governing the actions of the other characters.

5. Ask the class to break into small discussion groups of no more than four students per group. I usually allow students to form their own groups, intervening only when there appears to be a student hesitant to join a group or whom a group is hesitant to accept. I'm fully aware many collaborative-learning gurus advocate teachers assigning students to groups, claiming this is the only way to achieve heterogeneous groupings. However, I have found that students work better when they are allowed some freedom of choice—there are fewer complaints about the behavior of those in the group, and there are seldom students who are unable to fit into one of the groups. There may be circumstances, however, when it is best for the teacher to choose the members of each group; for instance, if you are aware of students who have already established strong opinions about a topic, you may want to arrange groups so that those students are not concentrated in one group. This would allow for a cleaner, more diverse discussion.

6. Once groups have been formed, give students the There Should Be a Law proposal form and allot enough time to complete the proposal, which they will present to the class. After the presentations, the class will vote on which laws to pass.

7. At the end of the allotted time, have each group give a proposal to the class. Once the presentations are complete, have a vote on which law to pass.

8. Arrange time at the end of the lesson for students to discuss the exercise. I begin by asking them what the hardest part of the lesson was.

Evaluation:

It could be very easy to negate progress made toward having meaningful discussions by giving some type of arbitrary grade for "participation." Some teachers have found this to be a very valid mechanism to ensure each student plays an active part in the discussion. However, I have found that it leads to empty student comments that are mere attempts at getting the "participation" points, so I try to stay away from that. Instead, I try to award points for meaningful participation, without my having to be the one solely responsible for determining what was meaningful. However, I usually try to give a base number of points (but never enough to pass) to anyone who gives the appearance of participating, and then I build in various ways to add additional points so that it takes real effort to make a top grade. You may want to consider some of the following:

- **Points for completion of individual work, such as the Evidence Organizer —** This can be done very quickly. For instance, as a part of roll call, ask to see their completed work, marking the points in your grade book as you go. This allows students to have their work graded yet still have it with them for the discussion.

- **Points for completed small group work, such as Law Proposal Sheet —** Again, this can be done very quickly. I usually ask to see the sheet at the beginning of each group's presentation. I enter the points into the grade book, and the group still has its sheet to use in the presentation.

- **Points for going Above and Beyond —** For example, each group may choose the one member who has contributed the most to their presentation, and that student is given the Above and Beyond points. Above and Beyond points could also be given to the group whose law was adopted.

Sample Rubric
"All the Years of Her Life"

Item	Point Value	Points Earned	Total
Participation in discussions	35		
Individual (Evidence Organizer)	35		
Group (Law Proposal)	10		
Above and Beyond for Group	10		
Above and Beyond for Class	10		

Comments:

Evidence Organizer

Character	Character's Actions	My Thoughts About This

Discussion Tracker

Student	Topic	Comments

There Should Be a Law

Law	Evidence
	From Story:
	From Life:

Lesson Three

Literature: "The Tell-Tale Heart" by Edgar Allan Poe

Strand: Justice/Suspense

Activity: Debate

Timeline: 1–2 days

Materials Needed: Evidence Chart
Debate Tracker

Learning Objectives: Students will (1) track and record evidence from the text; (2) participate in a debate; and (3) write a short paper using evidence from the debate and reading.

Lesson Summary: After the teacher has read the story to the class, students will track evidence found in the story to support their positions in a debate. Following the debate, students will write a short position paper.

Background Information

The Literature:

The story is narrated by a confessed murderer who is trying to convince the reader that the crime was justified. The narrator takes the reader through the days leading up to the murder, describing how it was planned and practiced. The actual murder is described, as well as its cover-up. When the police arrive to investigate unusual noises, the narrator confesses and points to the hiding place of the body.

This story is not only one of Poe's most famous, it is also one of the most frequently presented. There have been reproductions of it not only in many film and video anthologies commonly available to educators but also in many cartoons such as *The Simpsons*. The action is quick, the plot is suspenseful, and the premise is ripe for discussion and debate.

The Activity:

Although Poe's work is a favorite among students, I have found many of them have trouble with the vocabulary. This hesitancy with the words tends to slow down the action in this story, so I usually ask students to read their copies of the story silently as I read aloud. I tell the students that they will be debating an issue presented by the story, then I begin reading, speaking very softly and very rapidly. My initial reading of the story, two or three pages, takes no more than 10 minutes and is followed immediately by the question on which our debate is centered. If this is the first debate the class has had, I alert them to the rules for our debate.

Set-up: Desks should be arranged into three sections—a section to the right for those who support one side of the issue; a section to the left for those who support the other side; and a section in the middle for those who are undecided. Students move their own desks to the appropriate location just before the debate begins.

The Activity: Students are given Evidence Organizers on which to gather evidence from the story to support a position in the debate and are instructed to complete the chart before the debate.

Rules: Only students seated in a section supporting a position on the issue are allowed to speak. (This always means that the neutral area is overflowing at the beginning of the debate, but it dwindles.) Students can move from section to section as their opinions change.

Each side will have the chance to present ideas or evidence, one student at a time. For example, a student on one side presents a piece of evidence, and then a student from the other side presents a piece of evidence. Sides continue to present evidence in this way until all evidence is "on the table." I caution students not to respond to evidence with which they find an objection, but to note it on their Debate Tracker. This is when some of the undecided students begin to move from the middle. It is also a time when students move because they hear a piece of evidence they had not previously considered.

Once all the evidence has been presented, we follow the same procedure to present arguments against evidence. The sections become fluid as students switch sections as their positions change. Again, I caution students to write down anything they find noteworthy for use in their position papers.

Outcome/Decision: The decision is based purely on how many students are in each section at the end of the allotted time. The section with the most students wins the debate.

Although this is by no means a formal debate, I have found it to be immensely useful. It allows students to experience the reality of opinions—they are fluid and change as evidence is gathered and ideas, even opposing ideas, are thought through. Because the debate exposes students to the ideas and evidence of an opposing viewpoint, it also prepares them to write position papers that not only state a position, but support it and often refute the opposing view.

Lesson Outline:

1. Before reading the story to the class, tell students they will be debating an issue presented by the work. Once finished with the reading, present them the debate question: **Was the narrator male or female?**

2. Give students the Evidence Organizer and a set amount of time (usually overnight) to reread the story, note evidence, and take a position.

3. Before the debate, ask students to move their chairs into the appropriate locations for the debate and check the Evidence Organizers of those in each of the position sections.

4. As the debate takes place, students use a Debate Tracker to preserve noteworthy comments for later use. I often also jot notes on a Debate Tracker.

5. Once the debate is over, have students write a position paper, stating their ideas about the gender of the narrator.

Evaluation:

Students are familiar with being graded on a sliding scale of right/wrong. Teachers often assign essay questions that allow little room for true individual opinion, so students are familiar with trying to prove the teacher's ideas/opinions about a piece of literature. This lesson eliminates all of that. **There is no definitive evidence about the narrator's gender.** Of course, I never tell students this until after the position papers are returned to them and discussed.

So, how does one grade this lesson? The Evidence Organizer can serve as a grading mechanism. When completed, it documents students' attempts at finding evidence to support a position. You might require a certain number of citations, or you may want to simply give credit for completion. You may also want to build into the grading rubric the idea of grammar and punctuation.

If the lesson is followed by a position paper, you might include addressing citations as a requirement in your grading rubric. For instance, students could easily incorporate informal citations using page numbers and names gathered on their Evidence Organizer.

Sample Rubrics

Evidence Organizer

Item	Point Value	Points Earned	Total
Minimum number of citations	25		
Page numbers noted	25		
Position taken	25		
Correct punctuation	25		

Comments:

Position Paper

Item	Point Value	Points Earned	Total
Position clearly stated	30		
Position well-supported	40		
Citations from story	20		
Citations from debate	10		

Comments:

Student Name: _____

Evidence Organizer

Page No.	Evidence	Position Supported

Student Name: _____

Debate Tracker

Speaker	Comment	Position Supported

Lesson Four

Literature: "The Walrus and the Carpenter" by Lewis Carroll

Strand: Justice/Relationships

Activity: Mock Trial/Newspaper

Timeline: 2–3 days

Materials Needed: Lottery Slips
Jury Ballot
News Article Information*

Learning Objectives: Students will (1) participate in small groups preparing for trial; (2) simulate a trial for two characters in the poem; and (3) write a brief summary of the trial.

Lesson Summary: After reading the poem, students will draw lottery slips determining which part they have in the trial and then break into small groups to prepare for the trial. Following the trial, students will write summaries of the trial to be compiled into a newspaper format for distribution to the class.

Background Information

The Literature:

The themes of peer pressure, neglect of the young, and murder are hidden in the sing-song rhythm, clever word play, and unrealistic characters of this poem. A walrus and a carpenter come upon a bed of oysters and through the skillful use of peer pressure successfully lure the young oysters out of their oyster bed "for a walk," during which they kill and eat the young oysters. The only living witness, other than the walrus and the carpenter, is the eldest oyster who remains quietly in the oyster bed.

The Activity:

I have found that students love to argue, even if it means they must prepare to do so, and this lesson takes some preparation, both for the student and for the teacher. Despite this, the lesson is a valuable one, as students are able to experience a taste of our judicial system while also learning to look very closely at literature.

I caution teachers not to use a piece of literature filled with characters who could be witnesses in the trial. Because there are only three witnesses in this poem (the walrus, the carpenter, and the eldest oyster), it works well with the number of students I usually have in each class, which is around 30–35. (However, I have used this lesson with a class of 43 students and one where there were only 19 students.) I would also caution teachers to allow enough time for students to prepare adequately for the trial. Without enough time, students are apt to leave the courtroom action to a few aggressive classmates, defeating the purpose of allowing all of the students to participate.

Set-up: The day of the trial, there should be a witness stand and a judge's bench at the front of the room. Facing these, with their backs to the class, the prosecuting and defending attorneys need a space. The two defendants sit with their attorneys, and the jury should sit sequestered at one side. You may decide to have expert witnesses for each side, a bailiff, and a clerk. If you begin to run short of students to fill each group, you might have to find other teachers or administrators who are willing to play some role in the trial.

The Activity: Students will be working in small groups for each part in the trial. For example, there will be a small group preparing for the part of prosecuting attorney and another for the defense attorney. Although students draw to determine the group with which they will work, I do allow them the opportunity to exchange their parts provided they can find students willing to exchange and that they do so within the first few minutes of the drawing. Once parts have been drawn, groups begin working on strategies for the trial by studying the poem for clues and evidence.

It is in the groups that "actors" are elected. The group preparing the defense, for instance, elects one or two who actually play the part of the defense attorney. I intervene only when no one wants to role-play, something that seldom happens.

Rules: Students should not talk between groups and should keep their voices down, merely to protect their "sensitive" information. However, I tell them that the prosecution and the defense must eventually alert each other to their potential witness lists.

- The judge is responsible for introducing the case and for ruling on objections.

- There are opening statements given by the prosecution and then by the defense; however, the defense can choose to wait until after the prosecution has presented witnesses before giving their opening statement (few do).

- The prosecution then begins calling witnesses and is allowed to ask open-ended questions.

- The defense is allowed to cross-examine each witness, asking questions designed to make the jury suspect the integrity of the witnesses. Once the prosecution is finished presenting witnesses, the defense takes over. (They may now present their opening statement, if they have not already done so.) The defense calls witnesses and asks open-ended questions, and then the prosecution is allowed to cross-examine.

- When all of the witnesses have been questioned and cross-examined, the opposing sides give their closing arguments, with the prosecution going first. They can say anything they want, but they cannot introduce new evidence. The defense follows, and when finished, the prosecution is allowed a rebuttal.

- The judge instructs the jurors, reminding them of the charges, and the jury is sequestered until a decision is reached. Upon reaching a decision, the jury returns to the class and gives its decision to the court.

Lesson Outline:

1. Discuss with the class the rules and procedures of a mock trial before the literature is introduced.

2. After students read the poem, hold a lottery to create the small groups.

3. Students work in the small groups preparing for the trial.

4. Hold the trial.

5. Once the trial is over, allot time to discuss the experience.

6. Each group, or each student, must then write a news article about the trial that will be presented to the class. Provide students with sample news articles along with the News Article worksheet.

Evaluation:

There are many ways to document a grade from this exercise. One is to devise a small group activity worksheet, much like the There Should Be a Law proposal form in Lesson Two, that asks each group to track what it has learned (and from where) about its particular part in the trial. You could then attach a grade to the worksheet for each member of the group. You may want to attach an individual grade to a writing exercise. Give extra points based on the court's decision or on a class or group vote for Above and Beyond, again as in Lesson Two.

Sample Lottery

Jury Member	Jury Member	Jury Member	Jury Member
Jury Member	Jury Member	Jury Member	Jury Member
Jury Member	Jury Member	Jury Member	Jury Member
Prosecution	Prosecution	Prosecution	Prosecution
Defense	Defense	Defense	Defense
Defendant	Defendant	Defendant	Defendant
Defendant	Defendant	Witness	Witness
Witness	Witness	Witness	Witness
Clerk/Bailiff	Judge	Judge	Judge

Jury Ballot

We, the undersigned jury members, do find the defendant, (name of defendant) _____

Guilty   Not Guilty

of the crimes for which accused.

Jury Member #1 Signature:	Jury Member #7 Signature:
Jury Member #2 Signature:	Jury Member #8 Signature:
Jury Member #3 Signature:	Jury Member #9 Signature:
Jury Member #4 Signature:	Jury Member #10 Signature:
Jury Member #5 Signature:	Jury Member #11 Signature:
Jury Member #6 Signature:	Jury Member #12 Signature:

Signed by the Jury Foreman: _____

News Article

In writing your news article, you should remember to address the following points:

- Who?

- What?

- When?

- Where?

- Why?

- How?

Be sure to put the most important ideas or facts at the beginning of your article. You should include at least one direct quote in your article.

_____

_____

_____

_____

_____

_____

_____

_____

Chapter Three

Art, Movies, and Music

All life is a struggle in the dark.
—Lucretius, *On the Nature of the Universe*

By encompassing all that is around us, art (in its many forms) reflects who we are and allows us a glimpse of who we might be. This is one reason people love to read, using literature to look both inward and outward.

I have found that when students add other dimensions of art to reading literature, they gain the opportunity to experience a more accurate view of what the literature has to offer. For this reason, I try to build in ways for students to combine art created by others as well as what they have created themselves, based on the literature they are reading.

The art we view ranges from originals I borrow from local libraries to crayon drawings made by other students and other classes. I try to include art in all its forms, although I stay away from art that has subject matter obviously not consistent with the guidelines of the school district, eliminating art with overtly sexual content or with depictions of alcohol or drug consumption.

Sometimes we take calendar copies of "the classics" and cut them to pieces, and sometimes we take Play-Doh™ and make our own "classics." Students have listened to classical music that is tied to a contemporary piece of literature, and I have discovered that—when understood—some heavy metal lyrics are based on Greek mythology. And, through it all, we have made connections, tying other art forms to literature and tying the literature to our lives.

Lesson One

Literature:	"Flowers for Algernon" by Daniel Keyes
Strand:	Prejudice
Activity:	Calendar Cut-ups/Art Posters
Timeline:	1–2 days (prior to reading)
Materials Needed:	Calendar Cut-ups Art Posters* Questionnaire for Cut-ups Ladder of Prejudice (developed by Gordon Allport)
Learning Objectives:	Students will (1) participate in small groups to fill out questionnaires on cut-out; (2) participate individually to fill out questionnaires on poster; and (3) discuss the results of their decisions.
Lesson Summary:	Prior to reading the story, small groups of students will make and present to the class decisions concerning a person being depicted in a "calendar cut-up." Students will then individually make decisions about people in an art poster, followed by a discussion on prejudice. Finally, students will begin reading the story.

Background Information

The Literature:

The story "Flowers for Algernon" follows the diary entries of Charlie, a self-described "slow adult" as he undergoes an operation intended to increase his intelligence. The diary entries not only show a difference in Charlie's spelling and grammar as his intelligence rises but also show the difference in the way he is treated by those around him as his IQ initially rises and then eventually falls.

Although this selection does a wonderful job depicting the prejudice experienced by the mentally challenged, it can also easily lead to a discussion of other types of prejudice. This activity would work well with any piece of literature dealing with prejudice.

The Activity:

Set-up: Students should be able to move quickly from a seating arrangement that allows them to work in groups to one that allows for group presentations to the class, and finally to one that allows students to view art posters and to complete individual work. While the Art Poster section requires only that the teacher have access to posters (either by borrowing from a lending library or through his or her own purchase), the Calendar Cut-up section does require some teacher preparation. However, this is a preparation of materials that, if done properly, can be used from year to year.

Teacher Preparation:

Art Posters — The posters should depict people from various backgrounds in various settings. Teachers should arrange to have posters on hand either by purchasing three or four for use from year to year (be sure to laminate!) or by arranging for the use of three or four each year from a lending library.

Calendar Cut-ups — The preparation for this section may seem daunting, but the materials I have developed have served well from year to year. You will need some of those calendars that have a different piece of art for each month. Look for art that depicts various types of people, and be sure to have at least two copies of each picture you want to use. Calendars are very cheap at the end of the year, and occasionally I have received free calendars when I explained how I wanted to use them.

Once you have your calendars, you can follow these steps to prepare one cut-out for each group:

1. Have at least two copies of the same piece of art per cut-out. Once you have decided on the art, have each piece laminated.

2. Next, choose a central person in the art to carefully "cut out" of one of the copies. Attach a small piece of VELCRO® to the back of this cut-out.

3. On the copy of the art you *did not* cut, attach a small piece of VELCRO® to the front of the same person. This allows the materials to be stored for later use without losing pieces.

4. Do the same for each piece of art. Make sure you have enough cut-outs so that each group can have its own. You may want to use the same piece of art with each group, or you may want to vary the actual piece of art from group to group. I have found it is easier to find and make enough materials for the exercise if I vary the art.

Lesson Outline:

1. As the lesson begins, have students arrange their seating for small group work and give each group one cut-out character and one Calendar Cut-up Questionnaire. Each group then makes decisions about its character within the allotted time. I usually give the groups 10 minutes.

2. Each group shows its cut-out to the class and explains the reasoning behind the decisions it made in filling out the questionnaire.

3. Once all of the presentations have been made, show students the "whole picture" that matches the cut-out characters with which they have been working. At this time, you may choose to go directly to number 5, moving the students into a discussion of prejudice, or you may choose to continue with number 4.

4. Give students individual questionnaires and show them three or four new art posters that are displayed around the room. Each student should pick one of the posters to use in answering the Calendar Cut-up Questionnaire. After the allotted time, each poster is discussed by those who chose it for their questionnaires.

5. Next, have a classwide discussion. I use the Ladder of Prejudice as a transparency. In explaining his belief that prejudice comes in degrees, Gordon Allport developed the concept of a "ladder" of prejudice, with each step representing a degree of prejudice. Allport maintained that everyone is somewhere on the ladder. The steps of prejudice begin at the bottom with speech and rise in severity to the top rung of extermination. The following are some of the brief comments I make to the class in discussing this visual. For a more complete explanation read Allport's (1979) *The Nature of Prejudice.*

> **Speech:** Anyone who has ever told a racial joke (or heard one and laughed . . . or heard one and said nothing) is on the first step. I ask students to think about those "How many (*fill-in-the-blanks*) does it take to change a light bulb" jokes.

> **Avoidance:** Anyone who has ever wanted to stay away from "those types" is on the second step. Joining clubs or groups because there aren't any of "them" is an indication of avoidance.

> **Discrimination:** Anyone who wants to officially keep "them" away is on step three. The key difference between avoidance and discrimination is found in rules and regulations that prohibit "them" from belonging.

> **Physical Attack:** Anyone on the fourth step finds no remorse in attacking or destroying not only the property of "that group" but

also people who are in the group as well. Although it's easy to cite Germany's Night of Broken Glass or the South's lynchings as examples of this step, I've never had a year when I couldn't also cite examples from current newspapers.

Free Speech: I caution students to try to understand that, while seeming to criticize a basic principle of our form of government, this step represents the official sanction of the other steps. In other words, there is legal protection for anyone who gives a speech advocating discriminating against or harming "them."

Extermination: While Germany's systematic extermination of more than six million people during World War II is what led Allport to begin his research, the result is the caution that other countries have reached this step of the ladder as well. Our own country's treatment of Native Americans gave government sanction to those on this step. I also find it very easy to provide students with current news accounts of individuals, as well as nations, who are functioning on this level.

6. After explaining its basic concepts, ask the class to talk about any connections they see between the exercises they just finished and the information compiled by Allport. This usually leads to a discussion of the assumptions they made about the people in the cut-outs being based on limited information and while the posters provided more information, decisions were still made about the people based on external clues in the surroundings.

7. Finally, tell students the basic premise of the story and ask them to begin reading, noting for further discussion any connections between what occurs to and between characters in the story and what they experienced during the exercises.

Evaluation:
Since the intent of the lesson is to help students explore the nature of prejudice and to create an interest in reading the selection, you may want to forgo, or give minimal weight, to grading these sections. However, you could easily develop a grading rubric for the class presentations as well as for filling out the questionnaires. You might also consider developing a writing assignment based on the exercise.

Calendar Cut-up Questionnaire

1. What is this person's name? _____

2. Describe this person's home. _____
    _____
    _____

3. Describe this person's occupation. _____
    _____

4. What are his or her hobbies? _____
    _____

5. What does this person do with his or her friends on Wednesday night?
    _____
    _____

    Saturday night? _____
    _____

6. What type of food does this person like? _____
    _____

7. Where does this person like to travel? _____
    _____

8. What was the last thing this person read? _____
    _____

9. What type of music does he or she like best? _____
    _____

10. What is something his or her parents taught him or her? _____
    _____
    _____

11. What is something he or she would *never* do in public? _____
    _____
    _____

The Ladder of Prejudice
Developed by Gordon Allport

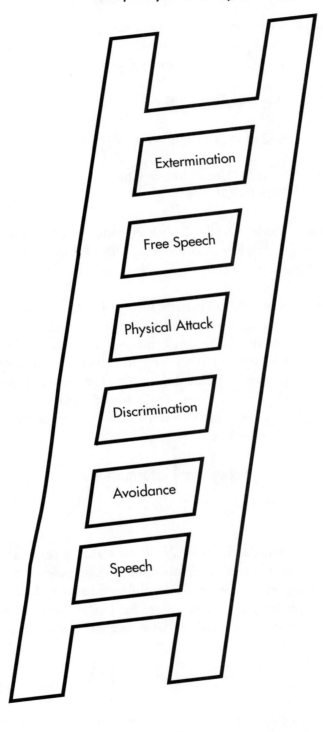

Extermination

Free Speech

Physical Attack

Discrimination

Avoidance

Speech

**According to Allport, everyone is somewhere on this ladder.
Where are you?**

Lesson Two

Literature:	*The Pearl* by John Steinbeck
Strand:	Prejudice/Heroes and Villains
Activity:	Play-Doh™ Decisions
Timeline:	1–2 days prior to reading and 1–2 days after reading
Materials Needed:	Hero/Villain Evidence Chart Play-Doh™*
Learning Objectives:	Students will (1) track evidence while reading; (2) participate in small and large group discussions; and (3) create a scene from the story.
Lesson Summary:	Students discuss the idea of heroes before reading the selection, and while reading they track evidence from the story for use in discussions centering on prejudice and heroes. After reading and discussing the story, students break into small groups to decide if the main character is a hero or a villain and then present their decision to the class, using Play-Doh™ to create an object or scene that was pivotal in their decision.

Background Information

The Literature:

The simple style of John Steinbeck's *The Pearl* makes it easily accessible to most students. The story is set in a small Mexican fishing village and tells what happens to Kino, a poor fisherman, who at first considers himself lucky to find "the pearl of the world." Through simple language, students are led to the complex issue of prejudice and whether a good man, motivated by what become less than good intentions, should be considered a hero.

The Activity:

While playing with clay may seem to be a very simple assignment, it is not easy. It requires students not only to process the story, but also to analyze and make judgments about all the various elements of the piece before making a decision about Kino, the main character. Then students need to be able to conceptualize their decision into one symbolic representation—made of Play-Doh™. Things are usually compounded when I give each group only two colors of clay, forcing them to adapt their ideas to those two colors or to organize with other groups and trade pinches of this color for that. This has led to some students giving others quick lessons on how to mix primary colors to get variations of secondary colors.

Set-up: While students are working with the clay, you may want to have some water and paper towels on hand to alleviate the numerous trips to wash hands. You may also want to consider having butcher paper on the work surfaces (using newspaper causes the clay to pick up the colors of the print, muddling the colors).

The Activity: Before breaking into small groups to discuss the story, students should have read the story, and also tracked evidence to bring to the group. I have found that it helps students if they have page numbers ready for their evidence, and, therefore, have adapted the tracker in this lesson (the Hero/Villain worksheet) for this purpose.

Lesson Outline:

1. Before reading the story, have a class discussion on what it means to be a hero or heroine, since both males and females can perform heroic deeds. Because I have found that most students want to start the discussion by naming people they consider heroes, both famous and unknown, I begin the discussion by asking students to develop a definition for the word hero.

2. Then tell students that the idea of hero/villain will be discussed after they have finished reading. Give them the Evidence Tracker (Hero/Villain worksheet) to use while reading. Ask them to record any evidence they find (along with the page number) of Kino acting either like a hero or a villain. For each piece of evidence they cite, they should determine whether the action was heroic or villainous.

3. After students finish reading the story, have them assemble into groups and, using their Hero/Villain worksheets, discuss their individual decisions about Kino, ultimately coming to a group decision.

4. When the group has decided whether Kino is a hero or villain, they then must decide how to represent *why*—using the Play-Doh™.

5. Each group then presents its decision to the class, along with its Play-Doh™ creation, which is left on display in the classroom for a few days.

Evaluation:

This exercise dovetails at the beginning and end of a longer piece of reading. It would be logical to use some sort of traditional grading system for the actual piece of literature, but I would be hard-pressed to judge Play-Doh™ creations on an "A–F" or "0–100" scale. If you feel uncomfortable doing that, perhaps you can find an administrator who would be willing to take on that task. I find the following system much easier to develop: students receive a numerical value for completion of their Hero/Villain worksheet and then for completion of a written summary of their group's decision. I also give the Above and Beyond points to one member of each group, setting the rubric as shown:

Sample Rubric
The Pearl

Item	Point Value	Points Earned	Total
Hero/Villain worksheet	60		
Group Summary	25		
Above and Beyond for Group	10		
Above and Beyond for Class	5		

Comments:

Student Name: _____

Hero/Villain

Page No.	Hero	Villain

Lesson Three

Literature: *The Pigman* by Paul Zindel

Strand: Values/Heroes and Villains

Activity: Develop a Character Book depicting the values of a character

Timeline: Varies depending on length of literature—(I usually spend around three weeks on *The Pigman*, depending on the number of activities we try to cover).

Materials Needed: Symbolism Worksheet/Transparency
Character Book Requirements
Character Tracker
Character Symbols and Signs
Character Symbol Decisions
Dinner Date Prompt
Compare/Contrast Character Worksheet

Learning Objectives: Students will (1) track and record evidence from text; (2) participate in small group discussions; (3) compile a Character Book based on the literature, worksheets, and discussions.

Lesson Summary: Students will track evidence about characters as they read the literature and then, using the evidence, will make decisions about one character. They will then discuss their decisions within small groups. Following the discussions, students will individually complete a Character Book.

Background Information

The Literature:

Paul Zindel's novel, *The Pigman*, is a story told by alternating narrators who say they simply want to "set the record straight" about what happened to an elderly man they befriended. In direct contrast with John's teenage bravado and chapters full of action, Lorraine is hesitant and insecure, analyzing each step leading up to the Pigman's death, filling her parts of the story with detailed descriptions and background information. In the end, these two teenagers present readers multi-layered characters who are troubled and unsure how their actions, seemingly so innocent, resulted in such tragedy.

Although the underlying plot of Zindel's novel is indeed tragic, the actual telling of the story is absolutely hilarious. This piece of literature always has students laughing out loud within the first five pages (even during silent reading) and is one classwide assignment they all finish reading, many of them far ahead of schedule. Through the use of characters that students can so readily identify with, Zindel slyly provides opportunities for discussions of parental relationships, of love, of the alienation of the young and the elderly, and of the fine gradations between good and evil.

I have found students understand the methods of characterization more fully if they can identify with characters first. For this reason, I always try to deal with the characterization aspect of the curriculum requirements with this story about the loneliness of an old man, told by John and Lorraine, two lonely teenagers.

The Activity:

Although the worksheets in this activity are parts leading to a whole (the Character Booklet), each worksheet can be used individually to introduce or reinforce the ideas of not only characters in a piece of literature but also of assigning values of good and evil to people and their actions. The worksheets can be completed during or after the reading. I prefer having students complete some of them during the lesson (Dinner Date) and some after (Character Symbols and Signs). I have also found it interesting to have students complete a worksheet during the lesson, and then give them the same worksheet after the lesson and let them note how their opinions have changed since completing the piece of literature. The ideas generated by the worksheets usually need some outlet other than just writing; therefore, I have incorporated small group discussion into the activity.

Although the worksheets were developed to use with this piece of literature, any of them could easily be used with a variety of literature focusing on characterization. For instance, asking a student to compare himself or herself to any literary character is an activity that can plug into most pieces of literature—from short stories to poetry, anything that contains characters. The activity makes the student focus not only on articulating particular aspects of a character, but also on how the student learned about the character. When students can cite evidence from literature to show why they think a character is morose or happy-go-lucky, they can understand characterization.

I have found it useful to begin the lesson by reviewing the elements of characterization with students, using the information below on a transparency or on a board.

Authors can tell us about characters in many ways:
- a description of the character;
- the character's actions;
- other characters' dialogue; and
- the narrator's direct words.

It is very useful to have an example or two of each type of characterization. In addition to showing students examples, I ask them to develop examples of their own, sometimes as a group activity. Whatever method you design, it is important that students understand what they should focus on when reading so their examples are accurate characterizations.

So that students can avoid having to backtrack, the Character Book should be explained and discussed before they begin reading. I usually tell them to be thoroughly prepared for writing a paper about one of the characters in the novel and to compile their ideas about one of the characters in a notebook. I explain that I will be giving them worksheets periodically that should be completed and stored in their Character Books. I have found showing them the actual rubric is the simplest way to cover the requirements and grading scale for the activity.

Lesson Outline:

1. Review characterization techniques and introduce the purpose and requirements of the Character Book.

2. After distributing copies of the Character Tracker, read the first four or five pages to the students, and then allow them to continue reading silently. Remind them to choose a character by the time they have finished the second chapter.

3. Every two to three days, give students worksheets requiring each student to make judgments within an allotted time, usually overnight, about the character he or she is tracking. Remind students to mark page numbers for use when discussing the worksheets with their groups.

4. After the allotted time, students meet in small groups to discuss their responses to the worksheets. If timely completion of the worksheets is a part of the rubric, ask to see the worksheets, and sometimes the trackers, prior to the grouping of students for discussion.

5. At the end of the activity, students should bind their Character Books and turn them in for a grade.

Evaluation:

This activity could easily be divided into parts, with each part graded, or the final product, a Character Book, could be given one grade. Whether you decide to grade the parts or the whole is not important, but it is important to alert students to the method you choose so they can plan their time and effort. I have had some students who take notes on plain paper, using their own method of shorthand and then transposing information onto the tracker for their Character Book later; but, if told the tracker would be checked each time they had small group activity, they would have quickly changed their methods of notation.

I find it useful to combine the part/whole grading process, weighing the part less. For example, after giving a worksheet, and before grouping students for discussion, I quickly (usually during roll call) ask to see their completed worksheets and their Character Trackers and give a check/minus grade. You may want to make this a grade scale of "0" (no work at all), "50" (only half-completed), or "100" (fully completed), or a similar variation. The point is not to spend much time on this step of the grading process, which is meant to give you a quick way to note any problems the class, or an individual student, is having with the assignment while there is still time to offer help. This method also gives procrastinators a needed nudge.

After the Character Book is completed and turned in, I use the following rubric to assign a grade.

Sample Rubric
Character Book

Item	Point Value	Points Earned	Total
Character Tracker	25		
Character Symbols and Signs	10		
Character Symbols and Decisions	10		
A Dinner Date	10		
Compare and Contrast	10		
Character Paper	35		

Character Tracker

Character Chosen:

Page No.	Characteristic	Evidence From Text

Character Symbols and Signs

Each character listed below has things that are important to him or her. Draw symbols for each of those things.

Character	Symbol
John	
Lorraine	
Norton	
Miss Reillen	
Mr. Conlan	
Bobo	
Mrs. Conlan	
Ms. Jensen	
Dennis	
Angelo Pignati	

Student Name: _____

Character Symbols and Decisions

Character Name: _____

Decide which option is more like your character. Be sure to give three reasons for each choice.

Is this character more like a circle or a square? _____
Why?

1. _____
2. _____
3. _____

Is this character more like a wedge or a wheel and axle? _____
Why?

1. _____
2. _____
3. _____

Is this character more like a noun or a verb? _____
Why?

1. _____
2. _____
3. _____

Is this character more like a hurricane or a tornado? _____
Why?

1. _____
2. _____
3. _____

Is this character more like a baseball or a hockey puck? _____
Why?

1. _____
2. _____
3. _____

A Dinner Date

Character Name: _____

If I could have dinner with one character in _____

I would select _____ . S/he would drive a(n) _____.

We would meet at the _____ restaurant. I would order _____ ,

and s/he would order_____. I would enjoy being with this person because

_____

We would talk about _____

and _____.

After dinner, we might see a movie like _____ , or we might

_____. I know this evening would _____

because _____

_____.

Character Comparison/Contrast

Character Name: _____

Write two detailed paragraphs. In the first paragraph, compare yourself to your character, and in the second, contrast yourself with the character.

I am like _____ in many ways._____

_____

_____

_____

_____

_____

_____

I am not like _____ because _____

_____

_____

_____

_____

_____

_____

Lesson Four

Literature:	"The Monkey's Paw" by W. W. Jacobs
Strand:	Values/Relationships
Activity:	Drama and Video
Timeline:	3 days–2 weeks
Materials Needed:	Instruction Sheet Evidence Tracker Storyboards Awards Audio/Video Equipment
Learning Objective:	Students will (1) track and record evidence from the text and (2) participate in small groups to produce a drama.
Lesson Summary:	While reading the story, students will track evidence for appropriate places, props, and sounds to use when working in small groups to produce an audio, video, or stage drama based on the reading selection.

Background Information

The Literature:

"The Monkey's Paw" follows the fate of Mr. and Mrs. White and their son Herbert, who think they have come into the possession of a lucky charm—an old monkey's paw. Not quite believing in the superstition of the paw, but wanting to use any luck it may bring, they laughingly wish for money. The story portrays their receipt of the mysterious paw, their hesitant wish, and the tragic granting of that wish with an eerie suspense. It is this suspense, with its foreshadowing of horror, that makes this selection ripe for student-produced drama.

The Activity:

I believe Shakespeare had a vision of teenagers that led to his famous line "All the world's a stage." It seems as though students, even the shyest, are in a constant search for a stage on which their particular talents can be spotlighted—somewhere they can *pretend.* This lesson allows students to exhibit some of their creativity while, at the same time learning some of the more difficult elements in the study of literature: mood and tone.

Through a careful reading of the story, students pick up enough evidence to be able to choose the appropriate sound and props to recreate the same feeling of suspense and eventual horror produced in the story. What better way to introduce new or difficult ideas (how mood and tone are created in literature) than to attach them to what students already know—movies and television? However, the process of moving from the known to the unknown can sometimes be time-consuming, so I have learned to have a flexible schedule for this activity which, depending on the students and the details they want in their projects, can take as little as 2 or 3 days or as much as 2 weeks.

Although it is very rewarding to watch students so interested in accuracy that they order "real artificial" blood from a Hollywood company, there comes a time when students must be prodded to finish their project even if it means the end result is not full-length feature quality. For this reason, I have found it best to give students a schedule that, allowing for some readjustment, calls for projects to be completed the day before winter or spring break, creating a self-imposed urgency to finish.

Lesson Outline:

1. Give students an Evidence Tracker (to use in noting appropriate times to use sounds and props in their drama) and the Instruction Sheet (which outlines their choices for the project and sets tentative deadlines).

2. After reading and tracking evidence to use in their decision-making, have students form small groups and begin the process of creating their dramas by first deciding which type they will produce (audio, video, or stage).

3. Once they have chosen a drama type, students then decide which props should be used and which sounds would be best with different parts of their scenes.

4. Next groups complete their storyboards, detailing how and when they will need props and sounds. Tell them to draw in each step in their production. For instance, if they are doing a stage performance, the squares are used to show how the characters move around the stage. If they are producing a video, each square represents a camera shot. This exercise encourages students to think of all of the pieces, or elements, that fit into the whole. They must consider that perhaps a character who is sitting on a couch on one side of a room must rise and walk to the fireplace at the other end of the room before he or she can throw something into it.

5. Groups then decide which places within the classroom to use for their production. If any places outside the classroom are needed, they should obtain the proper permission to use those places.

6. Finally, the groups begin the process of recording (audio/video) or rehearsing (stage).

7. Once all the groups are finished preparing their productions, there should be a day for each group to present its drama to the class and for the class to vote and give awards.

Evaluation:

Monitor this activity periodically so that students don't get bogged down in unnecessary details. I have found that periodically evaluating each group's progress also forces me to look beyond the "fun" and see what students actually are accomplishing. Individual grades are given based on the Evidence Tracker before students first meet in small groups. This allows me to gauge which students need a clearer understanding of the concepts involved in the project before they become lost in their groups. Although I look over the Evidence Trackers for understanding of the concept, I grade them for completion, remembering the purpose of this evaluation—to spot those who need additional help.

I also build in evaluations throughout the group process so that I can correct minor problems before they become major problems. For instance, I require groups to determine their drama type (audio/video/stage) within the first day of forming their groups. This eliminates the procrastinators and spotlights quarrelsome groups. Once again, I give credit for completion. However, when looking at each group's storyboard, I am not as quick to grade solely on completion.

I look very closely at the storyboards of each group because extra time spent here lessens the chance of problems during the actual production. I look for inconsistencies in their plots. For example, sometimes groups will focus on the highly dramatic and ignore the seemingly boring sections that contain the foreshadowing necessary to develop sufficient suspense. I look for ideas not easily achieved within the scope of our classroom. Many groups have been alerted to look for better places or better ways to produce their dramas. Storyboard grades are generally based on an "A–F" scale, and, since I have a detailed conference with each group about its storyboard before discussing grades, I have seldom had any problems with justifying grades.

I also grade on the actual production of each group's drama, using a rubric I have presented to the class during the introduction of the lesson. The rubric incorporates the ideas presented on the schedule and includes the opportunity for Above and Beyond points by winning awards for presentations. I often let students help generate a list of award ideas, and the awards tend to read like Academy Award categories: Best Actor, Best Actress, Best Script, Best Sound, and so forth.

Evidence Tracker

Sometimes a particular prop or sound can add to the meaning of a scene. For example, a person repeatedly tapping a pencil on a desk could show nervousness, while the sound of birds chirping could show peacefulness. As you read, look for ways the story could benefit from a particular sound or prop.

Page No.	What's happening in the story?	What sound would help?	What prop would help?

Instruction Sheet

Because your group will be making a drama based on the story, you will need to read it very carefully, looking for ways to present it to the class. Once you have finished reading and have completed the Evidence Tracker, your group will decide on the best method to use, plan out the drama using a storyboard, produce your drama, and, finally, present it to the class, which will vote on awards for various categories.

The Method: Your group can choose one of the following three methods to use in presenting its drama.

Audio — Your group can present a radio broadcast of one scene from the story. You will need to decide who will play each character and develop a script for that scene. Your group should also have sound effects and music to help listeners better understand what your drama is all about. Experiment with different sounds to find the ones that are best for your broadcast and then rehearse the script with the sounds and music. Then, record the drama and broadcast it to the class.

Video — Your group can present a TV broadcast of one scene from the story. You will need to decide who will play each part and develop a script for that scene. Your group should also decide where to record the setting of your scene and who will videotape your drama. You should think about props that can add to the meaning of your drama, and you should experiment with the use of lighting to add meaning. Once you have these things decided, rehearse your scene. Then record the scene and broadcast it to the class.

Stage — Your group can present a stage production of a scene from the story. You will need to decide who will play each part and develop a script for that scene. Your group should also decide where to stage your drama and which props to use to add meaning. You may also want to experiment with lighting, music, and sound effects. Once you have decided these things, rehearse your stage production. Your group will perform its stage production for the class.

Storyboard Outline

Award Certificates

Award Certificate

Date:_____

This award is presented to _____ for excellence

in _____ as evidenced by the support of the class.

Award Certificate

Date:_____

This award is presented to _____ for excellence

in _____ as evidenced by the support of the class.

Award Certificate

Date:_____

This award is presented to _____ for excellence

in _____ as evidenced by the support of the class.

Lesson Five

Literature: American Folk Tales such as Davy Crockett and Pecos Bill

Strand: Values/Customs

Activity: Music and Dance

Timeline: 1 day

Materials Needed: Recordings*
                         Dance Steps*

Learning Objectives: Students will (1) listen to music from the era of America's frontier and (2) participate in a square dance and a line dance.

Lesson Summary: Sometime during the reading of American Folk Tales, students will listen to music from the period of America's frontier movement and then will participate in dancing to that music.

Background Information

The Literature:

American Folk Tales, full of exaggeration and hyperbole, are stories that lead students first to laugh and then to question the reliability of the authors of the stories. There are always a few students who are perplexed by the idea of people sitting around campfires telling these tall tales, especially if the tales are based on real people. Therefore, I try to find ways to help students make the connection between the literature and their own lives by bringing not only some of the fantastical articles from supermarket tabloids but also by letting them compare the music and the dances of the American frontier to that of their own. This particular activity works best when the literature clearly indicates something about the frontier; however, it would not be hard to imagine matching the tall tales of Paul Bunyan to music, and perhaps dance, about logging and mining, or finding music and dance to match the tales about John Henry.

The Activity:

This activity, simple and straightforward, is based on students listening to music and then experiencing the dances that might have gone with that music. The only difficult part might be a hesitancy on the part of some students to participate in the dance sequence. I try to make this something more than "just dancing" by presenting the steps and then having the whole class practice them quickly in sequence, and since the actual "dancing" part is such a small part of the whole activity (and since we all look foolish doing unfamiliar steps) most students are willing to try. I do not force those who are not willing to dance.

Set-up: Other than ensuring each student can hear the music, there needs to be some set-up during the time students are listening. However, during the time the students are dancing, the classroom should be arranged so that as much floor space as possible is available, particularly if your dances require groups to form, such as square dancing. Students could easily move desks, chairs, and tables quickly prior to the activity.

Teacher Preparation:

Music — Unless you have access to some appropriate music in your own collection, or are thinking about buying some of your own, look for some of the wonderful music anthologies found in most school libraries. If none is available at your school, ask your school's librarian to try to track down just what you need at the local public library.

Dance — Your school library is also a good place to look for dance directions. If none is available at your school, look in the local public libraries. Although I originally only used square dancing for this activity, I have begun to add country line dancing after a student alerted me to the similarities. The directions are much easier to find, and it requires little in the way of grouping of students. However, I recommend beginning the lesson with a square dance.

Lesson Outline:

1. Discuss the similarities between American Tall Tales based on real people and the stories found in supermarket tabloids. Ask students to discuss what the Folk Tales might tell about the people who lived during that time. Then ask what the tabloid stories tell about us.

2. Next, ask students to listen to one type of music of the era of the American frontier and to contrast it to the music of today. I try to stress that, like now, different people liked different types of music. After listening to some of the frontier music, ask students to discuss what the people who listened to that music were like and to explain how they came to that conclusion.

3. Then ask students to arrange the room for the dance sequence. Without music, I go through the steps, referring to the directions so that students know that this is not something I've invented (and because I forget the steps from year to year).

4. Next, again without music, the students and I go through the steps.

5. Finally, with the music, we try to put the whole dance together, usually with hysterical results. Sometimes we go through the routine a second time.

6. Finish the activity by asking students to discuss what the music and the dance might say to us about the people of the American frontier and what the music and dance of our times might say about us.

Evaluation:

This simple, silly activity was developed so that students could experience the music and dance of the era in which the literature they were reading was written. Because of the nature of this exercise, I have never found a need to "evaluate" their performance. It would be practical, however, to evaluate their responses to a writing prompt focused on the influence of one means of expression (music) on another (literature).

Chapter Four

Games and Simulations

What we learn with pleasure, we never forget.
—Alfred Mercier

Like Alfred Mercier, I believe that "what we learn with pleasure, we never forget," so I try to make whatever I am doing, whatever the students are attempting, fun for all of us. One way I do this is through the use of games and simulations, which convey to students some of the issues found in the literature they are reading. It is always my hope that this vicarious experience will result in students having not just a quantity of knowledge about the literature at hand but also a deeper understanding of a difficult concept. Very often, not only are students able to understand a concept more fully when presented in game or simulation form, but their experience also serves as a learning tool for me.

Therefore, I urge you not only to present students with games or simulation projects, but to participate with them so that you can fine-tune the projects to your students. I have tried to present projects and games that are based on broad concepts and easily bent to fit a wide variety of literature. Do not hesitate to change rules that are cumbersome for your students or to adapt timelines to fit your schedule.

Lesson One

Literature:	*The Diary of Anne Frank*
Strand:	Values/Relationships
Activity:	Crosswords
Timeline:	1–2 days for activity
Materials Needed:	Crossword sheet
Learning Objectives:	Students will (1) track and record evidence in the story; (2) develop a crossword for class use; and (3) solve crosswords others have developed.
Lesson Summary:	Students individually develop crossword puzzles based on one character in the reading. After exchanging puzzles with others in the class, students try to solve the puzzles and identify the characters upon which the puzzles were based.

Background Information

The Literature:

This play, adapted from the diary entries of Anne Frank, recounts the experiences of two Jewish families in hiding from the Nazis during World War II. Through skillful attention to detail, Anne Frank was able to capture each person's character so precisely that audiences feel they know each person intimately. This instant identification with the characters only serves to intensify the horror felt when the hiding place is discovered at the end of the play.

The Activity:

Although the play uses the words of a young girl, there are instances where unfamiliar vocabulary is used; yet, I do not like giving out a set list of vocabulary to all students. Because I am reluctant to have the story's momentum interrupted with periodic vocabulary checks, I decided to allow students to develop their own vocabulary lists. Knowing how easily that could quickly become a non-thinking exercise, I decided to take the idea a step further and put a narrower focus on student-generated vocabulary lists, and I decided to make the exercise fun. The result was this crossword exercise.

While students are asked to develop lists of unfamiliar vocabulary words, I also ask them to center that vocabulary around one of the characters in the play. For instance, if a student decided to use Margot for this exercise, the vocabulary on his or her list should all point toward Margot's personality or actions in the play. Each word should be a clue to Margot's character.

Once students have created their vocabulary lists, they then present the words in the form of a crossword puzzle. To streamline the process, and to make each student's puzzle as easy to read as possible, I provide the crossword format. Since I began using this exercise, I have had a few students ask if they could use their personal computer programs to generate the crossword puzzle, and I always allow them to do so. The purpose of the sheet is to make formatting easier for them. Whether they use my sheet or a computer-generated format, they will still have to decide on the list of words and then tailor that list to the character they have chosen.

Lesson Outline:

1. Make students aware of the project before they begin reading the play and suggest that they begin keeping a list of the words they find difficult. Establish set times periodically throughout the reading to check their vocabulary lists and make sure students are aware of these check points. This not only prods those who tend to procrastinate, it also allows me to spot any problems particular students are having while there is still time to help them.

2. As students read, they make a list of words that are unfamiliar to them. Students are responsible for looking up the definitions of their own words. At the pre-established checkpoints, they should be able to show me their lists of words and the definitions they have found.

3. By the end of the reading, students should have picked the character on which to focus their crossword.

4. After finishing the reading, students select the words from their lists to use in their puzzle. This usually means some of their words are eliminated, and it sometimes means they must be able to understand their words well enough to adapt them to their particular character.

5. Students then develop their crossword puzzle, using their own vocabulary lists to give clues to one of the characters. The rules are simple: They cannot tell anyone which character they are using.

6. I collect the crosswords, and then I randomly pass them out to the class, making sure no student gets his or her own. Give students a set period of time to work the puzzle. (I usually try to give them enough time to work the puzzles in class.)

7. The point of the game is not just to work the puzzles but to also guess which character is being described. I have found the puzzles are not the simple 2-minute variety if students know a *small* prize (such as a candy bar or homework pass) is at stake.

8. Winners can be determined in many ways. You may choose to award a prize to the first one finished, to the first person finished for each character, or to the creator of the last one finished. I usually try to work in a way to recognize, or have the class recognize, the best puzzle.

Evaluation:

Having the class solve its own puzzles allows for a teacher-free evaluation, so I do not grade the finished product. However, I do look closely at the process used and give grades for that during the periodic checks. I sometimes require a set number of vocabulary words at each checkpoint and then grade for that number and for definitions. You may find ways to develop a rubric to incorporate whatever you want to focus on with your particular piece of reading. For instance, you may want students to list the page on which they found the word, to indicate which part of speech the word was in the sentence, or to create their own sentences with the word. Be sure students are aware of your requirements.

Crossword

Use the words from your vocabulary list to make up an original crossword puzzle based on one of the characters from the reading.

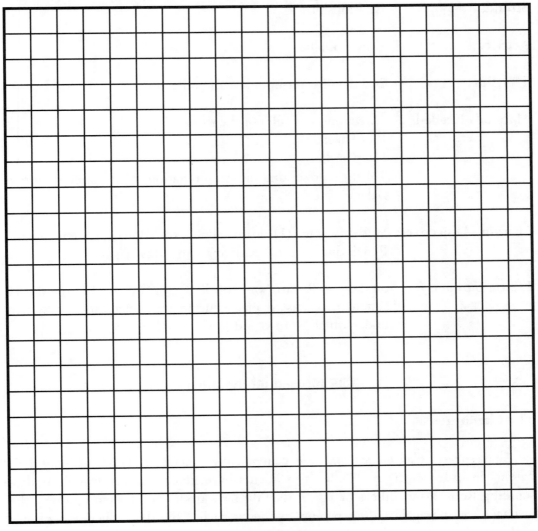

Across:

_____
_____
_____
_____
_____
_____
_____

Down:

_____
_____
_____
_____
_____
_____
_____

Lesson Two

Literature:	*Romeo and Juliet* by William Shakespeare
Strand:	Relationships
Activity:	Dowry Dollars
Timeline:	2–3 days for set-up, play, and reflection
Materials Needed:	Directions and rules of the game Fact Sheets Fate Cards Tokens representing the denominations of a monetary system Balance Sheets
Learning Objectives:	Students will (1) learn about the dowry system of the Renaissance and (2) participate in a dowry game.
Lesson Summary:	Students will learn some of the factors involved in the dowry system that was in place during the Renaissance, a system under which Romeo and Juliet found themselves.

Background Information

The Literature:

Shakespeare's play *Romeo and Juliet* centers to two teenagers who must defy their parents in order to marry. While my students have never had any trouble understanding Romeo and Juliet's defiance, they do have trouble understanding why the teenagers' acting against their parents' wishes is such a big deal. They also cannot understand the implications of Juliet's father's threat to turn her out to the streets.

The Activity:

The mention of dowries to today's students brings about giggles or blank stares. They have little awareness of how the practice of dowries restricted the opportunities and choices for women, and of how placing monetary values on women would undermine not only the women but also the men. While the dowry system was injurious to women, to allow students the ease of blaming it on "those ignorant, evil men of the time" would be an injustice. In developing this game, I tried to ensure that students would be exposed to how the requirement of a dowry affected how women and men perceived each other and themselves. The dowry system, as it was practiced during the Renaissance, represented an economic challenge to families and this game is based on that challenge. I hope that you allow students time for reflection, either oral or written, after the game.

Set-up: Divide students into groups or teams for this activity. For the maximum benefit, groups should contain males and females. Ask students to assume another gender for this game so that each experiences dowries from the opposite perspective. Use Fact Sheets to introduce the idea of the dowry systems and make them available during the game as a way to review.

Teacher Preparation: Have enough of the Directions and Rules, Fact Sheets, and Balance Sheets so that each group has its own copy and there are a few extra. Have Tokens, or their equivalents (perhaps poker chips) ready and Fate Cards prepared. I copy and laminate the Tokens and Fate Cards so that they can be reused in each class. However, I have found it best to file a copy to have on hand just in case something happens to pieces during play.

Lesson Outline:

1. Discuss the idea of dowries before the game begins. The Fact Sheet is a good basis for this discussion.

2. Divide students into groups or teams and give each team copies of the Directions and Rules. Explain and discuss the Directions and Rules so that all understand what is required to win.

3. Give each group the same amount of money and a Balance Sheet and begin the game according to the Directions and Rules.

4. Sometime during the game, students draw Fate Cards, which can affect the monetary situation of the team, and record these on the Balance Sheet.

5. Play the game for a set period of time before a winner (the team with the most money) is declared.

Directions for Play

Object: To protect and increase the family fortune while ensuring the matrimony, or its equivalent, of each member of the household.

Number of Players: Each group should have no more than five players. This will be your family.

Procedure:

1. At the beginning of the game, give each family the same amount of money.

2. Each family chooses a player to function as the patriarch. The patriarch does not have to marry.

3. During the game, the patriarch arranges marriages, or their equivalents, for each member of the family with a member from another family.

4. Each family has to draw a Fate Card.

5. All transactions must be noted on the Balance Sheet and signed by both patriarchs.

Winning: The family with the largest fortune at the end of the game wins.

Rules of the Game

1. Each family must have a patriarch. While families may discuss contracts, the decisions of patriarchs are final.

2. Balance Sheet transactions and contracts are to be done in ink. Once signed by both parties, they cannot be changed—only renegotiated.

3. Fate Cards cannot be traded and are to be honored by all families.

Fact Sheet

The following quoted material can be found in *Women of the Renaissance* by Margaret L. King (1991).

1. "From the instant of her birth, the prospect of a dowry loomed large over the female: she represented potential loss rather than potential gain."

2. "To manage the fearful cost of marrying a daughter, Florentine fathers had at their disposal a special institution: the *monte delle doti*, or 'dowry mountain,' an investment fund. Investing a reasonable sum at his daughter's birth or in her early childhood—the average age was five years, one month—a citizen could expect sufficient gain from a constantly reinvested yield to dower his daughter at an appropriate age. If the daughter died, the invested sum was lost."

3. "In fifteenth- and sixteenth-century Florence, girls were sent out at an early age as servants to patrons who took full responsibility for their keep and promised, after a set term of years, to release them with a dowry."

4. "The provision of a dowry for a destitute orphan or foundling girl was a principal act of charity."

5. "It was scarcely possible for a young woman not to marry. Social life did not include a category for the unmarried woman outside of the religious life."

6. "Chastity assured future husbands of the purity of their line, the legitimacy of their heirs, and the reputation of their family. Thus, the guarding of chastity was the primary business of the daughters of the Renaissance. Their honor consisted in the maintenance of their chastity; their fathers' honor consisted in their supervision of the chastity of their daughters and wives."

7. "Many Italian cities created institutions for penitent 'fallen' women, where through their own labor and benefactions they could hope for marriage (or monachation) and reentry to mainstream urban society … Many entered as young children, 'oblate' offered, with an emolument, to religious communities. 'Oblation' became a satisfactory means for the management of family resources. Gifts made upon entrance enriched the monastic foundation, which had reserves of manpower and managers to guard their wealth effectively."

8. "When wives died, they transmitted their wealth to their fathers' descendants who were also their husbands'. If a wife died childless, her dowry reverted to her natal family; the husband who had enjoyed its use was required to surrender it … The widow's family often had to work hard to recover the sum they had settled on their daughter, but the law was clear; it was rightly theirs."

9. "A daughter or widow without a father or husband would be assigned a guardian—a brother, an uncle, or any male at all—so that her property could be utilized; she alone was an insufficient instrument."

10. "While sometimes allowed to remain with her minor children under the authority of their father's heirs or executors, a widow and her dowry alike could also be recovered—'extracted'—and, as it were, recycled: she could marry again, as advantageously to her natal family as before. The children, necessarily, were left behind: they were the property of their father's lineage."

Tokens

You may copy this page for each family group, or use poker chips, with each color representing a different denomination.

1000 Ducats	1000 Ducats	1000 Ducats
500 Ducats	500 Ducats	500 Ducats
500 Ducats	500 Ducats	500 Ducats
100 Ducats	100 Ducats	100 Ducats
100 Ducats	100 Ducats	100 Ducats
100 Ducats	100 Ducats	100 Ducats
100 Ducats	100 Ducats	100 Ducats

Fate Cards

Cut the cards apart and then shuffle. Each family must draw a Fate Card, which represents experiences faced by families dealing with dowries. Numbers on the bottom-right of the cards correspond to the Fact Sheet.

Fate Card

Your family invested in the *monte delle doti,* which now funds the dowry of one of your daughters.

(2)

Fate Card

Your family invested **500 Ducats** in the *monte delle doti* at the birth of one of your daughters. She has died. **You lose your investment.** (2)

Fate Card

Your family generously provides a grant to the dowry of an orphan girl. **Lose 500 Ducats.**

(4)

Fate Card

Your family agrees to provide a village girl's upkeep and dowry for 10 years in exchange for her labor during that time. **Lose 500 Ducats.** (3)

Fate Card

There is some question concerning the chastity of the future bride of one of your sons. You are able to demand **500 Ducats more** in dowry. (6)

Fate Card

The plague has taken the life of your daughter's husband. She will return to your house with her dowry. **You gain 2000 Ducats.** (8)

Fate Card

The plague has taken the life of your daughter's husband. She, with her dowry, will remain in his father's household with her children. (8)

Fate Card

Fate has been good to your family, causing no economics.

Fate Card

Fate has been good to your family, causing no economics.

Fate Card

Fate has been good to your family, causing no economics.

Balance Sheet

Patriarch's Name: _____

Names of members in your household:

1. _____
2. _____
3. _____
4. _____
5. _____

Description of Transactions	Signature of Patriarch	Signature of Patriarch	List of Gains	List of Losses	Total
Beginning Balance	--------------	--------------	---------		

Lesson Three

Literature: *A Raisin in the Sun* by Lorraine Hansberry

Strand: Values/Relationships

Activity: Family Group Simulation

Timeline: 1–2 weeks (including reading the selection)

Materials Needed: Family Group Information Sheet
Balance Sheet
Job Application
Housing Application
Grocery Lists/Utility Sheet/Insurance Sheet
1–2 weeks' worth of newspapers*

Learning Objective: Students will participate in small groups simulating family units.

Lesson Summary: During the reading of the novel, students will break into "families." Each family will be responsible for finding jobs, securing housing, applying for insurance, paying bills, buying groceries, and facing an unforeseen crisis without running out of money by the end of the project.

Background Information

The Literature:

Lorraine Hansberry's play tells the story of a poor family. The mother, grown son and daughter, daughter-in-law, and grandson are faced with deciding how to spend $10,000 they are set to receive from the late father's life insurance. Each has different ideas and motives about how to spend this windfall.

The Activity:

I developed this activity as a way to involve students in making the types of economic decisions faced by every family so the students could better understand the interactions of the characters in the play. I have since decided to include the activity each year, even if it has to be tied to another piece of literature, because it is a powerful way for students to understand the ramifications of living with a set amount of income, helping them quickly discover the real meaning of *want* and *need*. This realization is well worth the time it has taken to develop the project so that now it is just a matter of securing enough copies of the various worksheets for each group, making sure students understand each phase of the project, and spot checking each group's progress.

Lesson Outline:

1. Before they begin reading the play, tell students about the project and the reasoning behind it. Make them aware of the dates and methods of grading at each checkpoint. Include the following statement on their unit planning information:

   "During this unit, the class will be divided into 'family groups.' Each family group will be expected to work within a budget and to save for the future. In order to do this, your group will need to complete a budget planning form. YOU NEED TO BEGIN SAVING CLASSIFIED SECTIONS OF THE NEWSPAPER NOW SO THAT YOU WILL HAVE THEM WHEN NEEDED FOR RESEARCH. Each 'family group' project will receive a grade based on completion of the project as well as amount of money saved."

2. Divide students into groups, form their "families," and give each group a Family Profile to fill out and turn in by the end of class.

3. Read and respond in writing to each Family Profile, creating some crisis that eliminates any sources of income. For example, a family who has a doctor finds upon reading the response that the doctor has lost his job, or the family depending upon an NFL football star's income finds that he's broken his legs and lost his contract.

4. Return the responses to the groups, then announce that each group must now look for work in the fields in which its members are qualified. To do this, they must fill out Job Applications and bring in classified ads for the jobs for which they are applying. (You may find it necessary to explain/review the way you want the applications to be filled out.)

5. Check over the applications, mark areas for improvement, and then return them to the groups with the information that the applications have been accepted, and that the jobs *all* pay $24,000 per year. (I use this number because it is easily divided by 12 making math simpler. Each group enters its income on its balance sheet.

6. In the next step, the students must find housing and are required to fill out a Housing Application (again, you may want to explain this process) and bring in a classified ad for the house or apartment for which they are applying. Check applications and either grant or deny housing. Reasons for denial vary from a rent or house payment that may be more than the family can afford to an incorrectly

filled-out application. (I allow students to redo applications if necessary.) Have each group enter its rent or mortgage payment on its Balance Sheet.

7. The next step can be as lengthy and detailed as your time allows. I refer to this section as *Bills,* and for my project, I include the following steps:

Utilities — Students fill out the worksheets on utilities, which are graded. The grade determines how much the utilities are for that family and the amount is entered by the family on the Balance Sheet.

Insurance — Give students an opportunity to apply for insurance for their home, car (if they elect to have one), possessions, and health. Each type of insurance requires a separate form, which you will check. Upon acceptance of the form, the amount of the insurance premiums is listed on the group's Balance Sheet.

Groceries — Each group is required to go "grocery shopping" sometime during the project. There are two ways to do this. One is to allow each group to determine what to "buy," and the other is to have a set list of purchases each group is required to make. I prefer to furnish a set list so students know the cost of buying balanced meals, including all the necessities as well as a few extra items such as potato chips. Otherwise, I have found that groups are likely to say their group does not eat much and spend an unrealistically low amount in this area. Whatever method is used, students are to bring in documentation of *real* prices. This can be advertisements in the paper or actual register receipts. Each group documents its grocery costs and posts this amount to the Balance Sheet.

Transportation — Ask students to decide on their family's method of transportation. This can be buying a new or used car or using public transportation. Then they fill out the worksheet on Transportation Costs and, after it is accepted, add their transportation costs to the Balance Sheet.

8. Next, each group participates in Family Roulette, which can mean additional income or unexpected loss to the family. One member of each family group draws a piece of paper out of a box and the result is posted to the Balance Sheet.

9. Balance Sheets are then tallied and, along with all of the worksheets and applications, turned in for a group grade on the project. Included in the packet from each group is the member the group has selected to get the Above and Beyond points.

10. As a way of reflection, both for the student and for me, I ask that students individually write about the exercise, explaining things that went well and those that did not. I am especially interested in how to improve the project for future students.

Evaluation:

I usually give a grade for the completed project that is shared by the group members (unless the group has indicated the member who deserves Above and Beyond points). The "grading" done on the worksheets and applications results in a positive or adverse effect on the group's Balance Sheet, so I do not enter it separately in a grade book. You may want to develop a rubric that weighs each aspect of the project or one that addresses only the group project that is turned in at the end. Be sure to share your decisions with the class at the beginning so they know what to expect.

Family Groups

Below, list the members of your group as well as a description of your "family."

Name	Age	Education	Relationship in Family
1.			
2.			
3.			
4.			
5.			

Write a paragraph in the space below that gives further information about your family.

_____

_____

_____

_____

_____

_____

_____

_____

_____

_____

_____

Budget Sheet

Rent/House Payment	$_____
Groceries	_____
Utilities	_____
Savings	_____
Investments	_____
Telephone ($25 basic plus long distance and extras)	_____
Newspaper	_____
Cable television ($30 basic plus $10/premium channel)	_____
Transportation	_____
Insurance Car	_____
House/Renters	_____
Possessions	_____
Health	_____
Clothes	_____
Haircuts	_____
Laundry/Dry Cleaners	_____
Entertainment	_____
Family Roulette	_____
Other (Specify) _____	_____

Total Expenses	$_____
Monthly Income	**$2,000.00**
Minus Expenses	- _____
BALANCE	$_____

Job Application

Name (Mr./Mrs./Miss/Ms.): _____

                                            Last   First   Middle

Current Address: _____

                           Street   City   State   Zip

Educational History: Begin with your most recent educational experience.

Name of Institution	Mailing Address	Course/Degree Year	Completed
Name of Institution	Mailing Address	Course/Degree Year	Completed
Name of Institution	Mailing Address	Course/Degree Year	Completed
Name of Institution	Mailing Address	Course/Degree Year	Completed

Employment History: Begin with your most recent place of employment.

Name/Address of Company	Dates of Employment	Position Held
Name/Phone Number of Immediate Supervisor	Highest Salary Earned	Reason Left
Name/Address of Company	Dates of Employment	Position Held
Name/Phone Number of Immediate Supervisor	Highest Salary Earned	Reason Left

Have you ever been convicted of a felony? _____ **Yes** _____ **No**
(If yes, explain _____)

(over, please)

Job Application - Page 2

References: List two references. Do not use relatives.

_____

Name   Address   Phone Number

_____

Name   Address   Phone Number

How did you find out about this job? _____

Can you operate any of the following equipment? Mark all that apply.

_____Computer - If yes, with which programs are you familiar?_____
_____

_____Calculator - If yes, with which functions are you familiar?_____
_____

_____Cash register - If yes, which types? _____

_____Other - Please specify. _____

What other skills/talents make you qualified for the job?_____
_____

Use the space below to write an essay explaining why you feel you are the best applicant for this position.

_____
_____
_____
_____
_____
_____
_____
_____
_____
_____
_____

Housing Application

Name (Mr./Mrs./Miss/Ms.): _____
                                   Last   First   Middle

Current Address: _____
                        Street   City   State   Zip

Employment History: Beginning with the most recent, list your employment for the last five years.

Name/Address of Company	Dates of Employment	Position Held

Name/Phone Number of Immediate Supervisor	Highest Salary Earned	Reason Left

---

Name/Address of Company	Dates of Employment	Position Held

Name/Phone Number of Immediate Supervisor	Highest Salary Earned	Reason Left

---

Name/Address of Company	Dates of Employment	Position Held

Name/Phone Number of Immediate Supervisor	Highest Salary Earned	Reason Left

Beginning with the most recent, list your place(s) of residence for the last five years.

Address	Own/Rent	Landlord/Phone No.

Address	Own/Rent	Landlord/Phone No.

Address	Own/Rent	Landlord/Phone No.

(over, please)

Housing Application - Page 2

Do you desire _____ 1 bedroom _____ 2 bedroom _____ 3 bedroom _____ 4 bedroom

List the names and relationships of any others who will be living in the residence:

_____
Name   Age   Relationship

_____
Name   Age   Relationship

_____
Name   Age   Relationship

_____
Name   Age   Relationship

List the make/model of the car(s) you or any other occupants of the residence drive:

_____
Vehicle Model   Make   Color   Year   Owner's Name

_____
Vehicle Model   Make   Color   Year   Owner's Name

_____
Vehicle Model   Make   Color   Year   Owner's Name

Have you ever been arrested? _____ Yes _____ No
If yes, explain. _____

Have you ever been convicted of a felony? _____ Yes _____ No
If yes, explain. _____

Do you own pets? If so, please list type and size. ($100 fee per pet) _____
_____

References: List two references. Do not use relatives.

_____
Name   Address   Phone Number

_____
Name   Address   Phone Number

Shopping List

Your family is now ready to go shopping. In order to document your purchases, you must either attach advertisements with the prices to this form or you must furnish a sales receipt indicating the item and price. Please indicate in the space provided the type/brand of product purchased. Also, list the store from which the purchase was made.

Item	Description	Unit Price	Total Price
2 dozen eggs			
1 gallon of milk			
1 gallon of skim milk			
8 oz. Cheddar cheese			
3 lb. ground beef			
1 whole roasting chicken			
2 frozen pizzas			
1 lb. sirloin tips			
1 8 oz. package of pasta			
3 cans of cut green beans			
1 loaf of bread			
1 package hamburger buns			
1 box of cereal			
1 2-roll package paper towels			
1 6-roll package toilet paper			
1 16 oz. package lunch meat			
2 bars bath soap			
1 box laundry detergent			
1 bottle shampoo			
1 tube toothpaste			
1 toothbrush			
1 head of lettuce			
1 package carrots			
5 lb. bag of potatoes			
2 onions			
4 navel oranges			
3 bananas			
2 tomatoes			
1 bottle salad dressing			
1 1 lb. bag of potato chips			
2 six packs of soft drinks			
1 pair of tennis shoes			
1 pair blue jeans			
		Subtotal	
		Tax	
		TOTAL	

Medical Insurance

Someone in your family has suddenly had an accident, and you need to apply for help. Read the Insurance Terms so that you understand how they are used in the form, and read the information about the accident. Then fill out the application.

Insurance Terms

Apt.	abbreviation for apartment
Assistance	help; money to help with costs and expenses
Benefits	extra advantages or extra money; special services
Completing	finishing; filling in all the items
Describe	tell about
Disability	illness or condition that keeps you from working
Eligible; eligibility	being suitable, qualified; allowed to receive
Include	put in; add
Notified	to be told about
Physical	dealing with the body
Prevented	stopped from doing
Promptly	immediately
Rec'd.	abbreviation for received
Relationship	family connection

Background Information

A member of your family has had an accident and is now unable to walk. Her name is Jane Ann Blackburn, and she is an aunt who lives with you. She was born on May 31, 1952. As a result of the accident, she will not be able to work for at least one year. She gets $100 per month from Social Security (her number is 251-93-1982) because of her accident.

Application for Medical Assistance

Please print or type. If you would like help in completing the form, you may either call or come in person to the address shown below. A staff member will be glad to help. You will be notified promptly about your eligibility for medical assistance.

<table>
<tr>
<td colspan="2">Please fill in all items and take or mail to:

52 State Street
Anytown, USA 00000</td>
<td colspan="2">For Office Use Only:

Record Number: _____
Record Name: _____
County/District: _____ Date Appl. Rec'd: _____</td>
</tr>
</table>

A. I AM APPLYING FOR MEDICAL ASSISTANCE FOR THE PERSONS LISTED BELOW.

Name (Last, First, Middle)	Relationship to Head of Family	Date of Birth (month/day/year)	Social Security No. or Medicare No.
Head of Family			

Family's Address (Street/Apt. No./City/State/Zip Code)

Area Code and Telephone No.

ANSWER ALL QUESTIONS FOR PERSONS LISTED ABOVE

B. Does anyone have any physical or mental disabilities that have prevented him/her from working during the past 12 months or that will prevent him/her from working in the next 12 months? ____ Yes ____ No

If "yes" enter here	Name	Describe Disability	Date Started

If "yes" enter here	Name	Describe Disability	Date Started

C. Does anyone receive Social Security disability benefits? ____ Yes ____ No

If "yes" enter here	Name	Describe Disability	Date Started

Utilities

Look carefully at the utility bill below. Do you understand it? If you don't understand how to read a utility or telephone bill correctly, you won't know if you are being overcharged. Even big companies sometimes make mistakes. It is important to know the different terms and figures on bills, and this exercise will give you practice in that. First, look at the copy of the utility bill. If your group wishes to use another type of utility bill, just attach it to this worksheet. Next, you will need to look at the vocabulary for words or abbreviations that might be confusing to you. Finally, using your utility bill, answer the questions at the end of the worksheet.

LOT 11 CEDAR BLK C
ACCOUNT NUMBER: 719-2210-04-0

MESSAGES

Your "Current Bill" amount of **$122.81** is due by **March 17, 1997.**

BILLING SUMMARY

Current Meter Reading (02/13/97)	37153
Previous Meter Reading (01/15/97)	-35641
Kilowatt-hours Used	1512
Energy Charge (1512 kwh)	$115.31
Base Customer Charge	$7.50
Current Bill	$122.81

Your electricity use

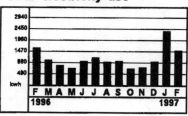
1996   1997

Total Amount Due   **$122.81**

Meter Number: 000032847
Rate: Residential Service (050)
Energy Charge Includes:
 Power Cost Recovery Factor: $0.0186765 per Metered kwh

For information call us at: (818) 555-0055

Your average daily electrical cost was $4.23

 Southwestern Electric Service Company
a Subsidiary of Texas Utilities Company

KEEP THIS PORTION FOR YOUR RECORDS
C0028860   022897

Vocabulary

Account number	the number given to you by the company to identify you and your account
Balance	the amount of money to be paid
Disregard	ignore
Kilowatts	amount of electricity used
Meter	machine that keeps a record of how much electricity (or gas) you use
Previous	earlier
Reading	checking the meter for the amount of electricity (or gas) used

1. When is payment due for this bill?_____

   _____

2. What is the total amount of this bill? _____

   _____

3. How many kilowatt-hours were used for this bill? _____

   _____

4. What is the customer charge included on this bill?_____

   _____

5. What is the account number for this bill? _____

   _____

6. If you have a question about this bill, who should you call? What is the telephone number?_____

   _____

Family Roulette

You won $100 in an out-of-state lottery game.

You caused a car accident. If your family has car insurance, pay a $200 deductible to repair the car. if your family does not have insurance, you must pay the total $950 to have the car repaired.

This was a normal week—no gains and no losses.

This was a normal week—no gains and no losses.

This was a normal week—no gains and no losses.

You were given a speeding ticket and must pay $100.

A birthday card arrived for you from a seldom-seen uncle. Inside was a check for $200.

If your family made investments, there was a gain of $200.

If your family made investments, there was a loss of $200.

There was an unexpected bonus in your paycheck of $100.

You sold some of your junk at a yard sale making $25.

If your family has a car, it needs repairs. Total cost is $100.

New coats are needed for all family members. Multiply the number in your family by the thrift shop price of $10.

Your family had an unexpected trip to the emergency room. If your family has health insurance, pay $100. If you do not, pay $800.

Your family received an income tax return of $100.

Your family received notification from the IRS that you owe an additional $100 in back taxes.

Lesson Four

Literature: Poetry Selections

Strand: Customs

Activity: Newspaper/Magazine Simulation

Timeline: Approximately 2 weeks, including reading time

Materials Needed: Instruction Sheet
Research Tracker
Record Keeper

Learning Objectives: Students will (1) individually research a topic for the group's project and (2) participate in small groups producing a newspaper or magazine.

Lesson Summary: As part of reading the poetry for a unit, students research topics related to that poetry and then, working in small groups, compile their research into a newspaper or magazine format.

Background Information

The Literature:

I have used this project as part of a unit on poetry. It works particularly well when the poetry is from a specific era or centered on a specific topic. For instance, the project would work if the poetry were from the Early Colonial period or from the Renaissance, or if it were poetry from different periods centered on the topic of war or love. The project would also be appropriate for any genre of literature, perhaps short stories or plays. The only real requirement for literature is that it be easily accessible to all the students as they will be doing a lot of the reading on their own.

The Activity:

The purpose of this project is three-fold. First, I want students to understand that there can be many interpretations of a piece of poetry. This can be accomplished through the student research as well as the student interaction in producing a group project. Second, students are self-directed (as much as students can be) in their research because, for the most part, the students determine what they need to learn in their research. Finally, the project gives students a hands-on demonstration in using different types of writing and allows them to practice the nuances of deciding which type to use for which purpose. It is this final purpose that is the most important during this project, and that is what I stress during the introduction of the activity.

I plan this project for *after* students have had other experiences with cooperative learning within the classroom so that they are familiar and comfortable with the process of working together. Since much of the project is self-directed (and it is impossible for me to be everywhere in the library at once), it is important that they understand not only how to work together, but how to solve the inevitable problems that can arise. By the time we begin this activity, students tend to rely on me simply as a sounding board, someone who is there to help them clarify their ideas or perhaps point them in the right direction.

Set-up: Give students the Instruction Sheets and divide them into groups at the beginning of the unit. Time, previously scheduled, is spent in the library only after groups have had a day or two to focus on what they want to learn while they are there. During the time they are still trying to pinpoint the focus of their library work, I ask each group to keep a record of what they are thinking about doing (and what they decide) and to leave the record with me at the end of each class period. This is so I can spot problems such as unrealistic expectations and also so the record does not wind up at home with a sick group member.

Teacher Preparation: Be clear in what you want to accomplish with this simulation. Your instructions to the students and your grading mechanism should reflect your focus, whether it be student research, the final product, or the entire process. I tend to focus on each aspect of the project in varying degrees, and this sometimes changes from year to year (and class to class). I have developed a rubric that acknowledges each part of the project, and I adjust the weight of the various items to fit the focus for the particular class.

It is also very helpful to have information available in the classroom about the various ways to make a booklet (if they are doing a magazine); examples of clip art they can use; art supplies, such as crayons and markers; different types of paper including construction paper; as well as rulers, scissors, glue, tape, and a computer or two.

Since part of the project requires students to have enough copies of their product for each group in the class, I also try to schedule time with the office secretary (or whoever is in charge of the copy machine) to copy the students' work.

Lesson Outline:

1. Give students a schedule for the unit that includes planning days, library days, production days, and presentation days. Included on the schedule is a list of the literature they can choose from and also will be responsible for on a standard Unit Test. List the date of the Unit Test on the schedule, also.

2. Give each student an Instruction Sheet and have the class discuss the requirements

of the project. It is important that you give sufficient time so students are clear on what is expected of them and on how they will be graded.

3. Form groups and then begin the planning stage. During this phase, groups make decisions about how their group is to function (they may decide to elect an editor-in-chief), which type of project they will produce (newspaper or magazine), and what to focus on during their time in the library. The decisions they make are kept on a Record Keeper that is left in the classroom each day.

4. The next step is for groups to spend a day or two in the library gathering information needed for their product. During this time, students are to keep *individual* Research Trackers that they leave with the teacher at the end of each day.

5. Upon returning to the classroom, groups begin the production phase of the activity. During this step, students write their individual articles, prepare any features such as cartoons, artwork, crossword puzzles, advertisements, and filler articles, and compile their work into the finished format. On the scheduled date, groups turn in their products to be copied. I usually schedule this so that groups have their copies back for at least one full class period before presentations begin.

6. The final step is distribution. Each group gives a copy of its work to every other group in the room (and one to me). You may want to plan a formal presentation. Just remember to give the groups enough time to look at the work of others.

Evaluation:

I use individual and group grades for this project, and usually record both on a rubric for each student. Students are graded individually on their Research Tracker and on the Unit Test, and as a group on the Record Keeper and final product. I also give groups a chance to award Above and Beyond points and for the class to give those points to one group.

Information to Include on Schedule:

Introduction	1 day
Planning days	2 days
Library days	2 days—with individual group members allowed to go for additional information
Production days	4–5 days
Date to turn in copy material	
Date copies will be returned	(students may spend time in between studying for the Unit Test)
Date for distribution	1 day (determine Above and Beyond grades)
Discussion of activity	
Unit Test	

Instruction Sheet

During the course of this unit, you will be working with a group of students to produce either a newspaper or a magazine that centers on some aspect of what you are reading. For example, your group may decide to produce a newspaper depicting the time in which the literature was written or the time used in the setting of the literature. Your group may decide to produce a magazine that is marketed to appeal to the type of people in the literature you are reading or centered on one of the topics of the readings. The choice is up to your group.

Once your group decides what it wants to produce, go to the library and search for the information your particular group needs. Each one of you will be required to write an article for your newspaper/magazine and you will need to prepare for it. For example, you may be writing an article about the mode of transportation during the era your group has decided to portray, and you need information about that (and possibly a photo or drawing of it). You may also need information about something extra you are doing, such as graphics. Since your group will have only 2 days in the library, it is important that you know what information you need. While in the library, you will be required to keep a Research Tracker for the work you are doing.

When the class returns from the library, each member in your group will write his or her article. Your group is responsible for proofreading and editing the articles in your publication. Once you are all happy with the articles, you need to decide how to compile them into your publication. Which ones will be the main, front-page articles? Which one should be used as an editorial? As a feature? Your group can also include any of the following in your publication: crossword puzzles, artwork, cartoons, advertisements, or short articles. If the group decides to use any of these, you will need to decide where to place them in the publication.

Your group will need to have any material you need copied for your publication ready by the deadline. Once copies have been made, you will have a day to compile the issue and have one copy ready for each group in the room (and one for your teacher). When this is done, each group will distribute its publication to the other groups.

Remember, you will be receiving individual and group grades during this unit. You and your group need to be careful to follow the schedule so you do not get behind.

Schedule

Date	Item
	Introduction: Be sure you understand what is expected of you.
	Planning: Make decisions and fill out Record Keeper.
	Library: Find information and keep a Research Tracker.
	Production: Write articles and develop your publication.
	Deadline for Copies: Turn in materials to be copied.
	Copies Returned: Your last chance to polish your publication.
	Distribution/Discussion: Determine Above and Beyond points.
	Unit Test: You will be tested on the literature in this unit.

Record Keeper

Make the following decisions during the planning phase.

Choice	Decision
Type of publication (newspaper/magazine)	
Name and focus or theme of publication	
Article/Author	
Article/Author	
Article/Author	
Article/Author	
Article/Author	
Artwork/Graphics	
Puzzles	
Advertisements	
Short Articles	
Cartoons	

Student Name: _____

Research Tracker

Decide what type of information you need before going to the library and list it here:

_____
_____
_____
_____
_____
_____
_____

Now, track all the places you look for that information in the chart below. If you decide you need additional information, you may include it on the tracker.

Information Needed	Source Checked	Information Found

Chapter Five

Reports and Research

The direction in which education starts a man will determine his future life.
—Plato, *The Republic*

One of the hardest things for any teacher to contemplate is assigning reports and research papers. It's not that we don't know how to approach these activities, or that we lack topics—it's usually that we dread the mountains of paperwork these particular activities generate. Yet, of all the possible learning activities that could occur in our classrooms, these are the two that are frequently a part of the "required curriculum." These are the two seen as the way to train students to seek information, to be the self-learners we all want them to be, and with the right emphasis these activities can be just that, without generating mounds of papers to grade.

Because the nature of this chapter is to present report and research activities that can be used generically, I have not included the **Literature** and **Strand** section in each lesson, focusing less on the reading material (you should be able to use any) and more on the method and activity.

Lesson One

Activity: Book Reports

Timeline: 1–2 days in addition to reading time

Materials Needed: Book Proposals
                         Book Report Forms

Learning Objectives: Students will (1) read a book with their parents and (2) report on the book.

Lesson Summary: After reading a book, students will complete a report on it.

The Activity:

I try to have students complete at least one book-length work during each grading period, alternating between teacher-assigned books (required by curriculum mandates) and those times when students choose their own. The format students use to report on their books also changes, varying from 1-minute oral reports to formal, written reports, although I tend to stay somewhere in between these two extremes. I have found that varying the method of grading reports made on such assignments keeps the students (and myself) from dreading them. This activity is based on allowing students to choose a book to read and on involving parents. Too often I have heard parents comment that they weren't sure what their children were doing in school or they only heard about the children's work and progress when there was bad news.

This exercise is a way of involving parents in the academic life of their children, and also a way of giving them an opportunity to have a reason to set aside time to talk with their children. Although I have had many positive comments from parents for "forcing" this interaction, there have been a few times when parental involvement was not possible. At those times, I allow the student to choose any adult he or she sees on a regular basis. These students have always been able to find someone they see outside of school (which reinforces the idea that people outside of the academic setting can find meaning in reading) for this project, but if this had not been possible, I would have allowed the students to use another teacher or an administrator at the school.

Lesson Outline:

1. Give students Book Proposals to fill out and turn in for the book they want to read. These proposals detail the format of the book report, when the report is due, and how the report will be graded.

2. Once the Proposal has been accepted, students begin reading and preparing their reports.

3. Students turn in their reports on the assigned day.

Evaluation:

I design a rubric based on the points outlined in the proposal. The rubric changes to fit the focus of each particular assignment. It weighs efforts in answering the questions with reasons based on the literature as well as in using correct punctuation and grammar. Points are usually given for completion of the assignment.

Book Proposal

You and your parents are to choose a book for this report. The book should be fiction, at least 100 pages long, and written on grade level or above. Once you have chosen the book, fill out the proposal, and turn it in to me. It is due on _____. You should then begin reading. After reading the book, both you and your parents should fill out a Book Report Form and turn it in for a grade. The report form is due by _____ .

Title of book you are proposing to read for this unit, including author's name:

_____

On the lines below, you and your parents should each write a paragraph on why you have chosen this book.

Student: _____

_____

_____

_____

_____

_____

_____

Parent: _____

_____

_____

_____

_____

_____

_____

In proposing and contracting to read this book for this unit, you are agreeing to the following:

1. You have not already read this book.
2. You will be responsible for obtaining a copy of the book.
3. You will have your copy of the book in class each day.

Student Signature: _____ **Date:**_____

Parent Signature: _____ **Date:**_____

Book Report Form

Answer the following questions using complete sentences. If you need more space, you may use additional paper and attach it to this form.

1. Who or what was your favorite character in the book? Why?

   Student: _____
   _____
   _____

   Parent: _____
   _____
   _____

2. What do you consider the book's main theme or message to be? Why?

   Student: _____
   _____
   _____

   Parent: _____
   _____
   _____

3. If you could change anything about the book, what would it be? Why?

   Student: _____
   _____
   _____

   Parent: _____
   _____
   _____

4. To whom would you recommend this book? Why?

   Student: _____
   _____
   _____

   Parent: _____
   _____
   _____

Lesson Two

Activity: Short Library Reports/Individual

Timeline: 2 days

Materials Needed: Assignment Sheet

Learning Objectives: Students will (1) research a topic in the library and (2) fill out a questionnaire about the topic.

Lesson Summary: Before going to the library, students are given individual topics and a questionnaire to fill out about their research on that topic. Upon returning to the classroom, they report their findings to the class and turn in their questionnaires for a grade.

The Activity:

This activity was originally developed to use with *A Raisin in the Sun*, a play about a poor family trying to decide how to spend an inheritance. One family member wanted to buy a house, one wanted to start a business—all faced prejudice. It was a wonderful piece, but our time in the library was scheduled to occur right in the middle of the story, and I had yet to include a student research project for that grading period. From that turmoil, I developed this quick research activity.

I have since used the same process for other topics and other pieces of literature, and I am confident you will be able to adapt it to your classes as well.

Lesson Outline:

1. Give each student a different topic, each related to a larger, broader topic, to research and a questionnaire to fill out based on what he or she finds during the research.

2. Then, students go to the library to find information on their topic, filling out the questionnaires as they go along.

3. Upon returning to the classroom, usually the day after the library trip, students give brief oral reports on their findings, giving the teacher the completed questionnaires after the reports.

Evaluation:

The intent of this activity is not to have students produce a long, formal report but to have them experience finding information quickly, reading and digesting it, and then summarizing it for the class. Therefore, I grade only the completion of the questionnaire, and I am very liberal on that since some topics have not lent themselves well to each question.

Sample Topics for
A Raisin in the Sun

1. What are possible reasons for the riots in Watts (1965)? What were any results or outcomes of these riots?

2. How much money does the start-up of the average small business require? What is the average yearly income for a small business owner in the U.S.?

3. What reason is given for the failure of the majority of small businesses? What might a future business owner do to prevent this?

4. How many new businesses are started each year in the U.S.? How many are still in business after 3 years? Five years? Ten years?

5. Explain the reasons some people oppose abortion and some people favor it.

6. What is the significance of The Civil Rights Act of 1957?

7. What is the significance of The Civil Rights Act of 1964?

8. What is the significance of The Civil Rights Act of 1968?

9. When was the Civil Rights Commission formed? What does it do?

10. What brought about the case *Brown v. Board of Education* (1954)? What were the results?

11. What brought about what is known as the Bakke Case (1978)? What were the results?

12. What caused the case *Swann v. Charlotte-Mecklenburg* (1971)? What were the results?

13. What brought about the case *Rotary International v. Rotary Club of Duarte* (1987)? What were the results?

14. What is the average purchase price of a single family home in the U.S.? In this state?

15. How does one qualify for an FHA loan? What type of down payment is required?

16. Who qualifies for a VA housing loan? What type of down payment is required?

17. Who qualifies for conventional home loans from a bank? What type of down payment is required?

18. What is the average family income in the U.S.? In this state?

19. Which professions are seen as the top "growth" professions in the next decade?

20. What is the average family size in the U.S.? In this state? Who heads the most households?

21. What is the educational level of the majority of heads of households in the U.S.? In this state?

22. Explain the significance of *Roe v. Wade* (1973).

23. What else has Lorraine Hansberry written?

24. Find another of Langston Hughes' poems to share with the class.

25. What was the reaction to *A Raisin in the Sun* when it first opened on Broadway?

26. Martin Luther King's "I Have a Dream" speech is now considered a piece of literature. What have literary critics had to say about this?

Research Questionnaire

Information/question you are researching: _____

_____

_____

_____

_____

Title of your source: _____

Written by: _____

Published by: _____

Publication Date: _____

Write a brief summary of the information you found: _____

_____

_____

_____

_____

_____

_____

Title of your source: _____

Written by: _____

Published by: _____

Publication Date: _____

Write a brief summary of the information you found: _____

_____

_____

_____

_____

_____

_____

Lesson Three

Activity: Short Library Reports/Groups

Timeline: 3–4 days

Materials Needed: Research Planners
                           Questionnaire

Learning Objectives: Students will (1) work in small groups to research a topic and (2) report their findings to the class.

Lesson Summary: The focus of this lesson is to do research in groups rather than individually. Students will divide into small groups and each group will be given a different topic to research in the library. After returning from the library, each group will present its findings to the class.

Lesson Outline:

1. Divide students into small groups and give them topics and Research Planners. Each group divides the work to be completed among its members. For instance, a group may decide to break the topic into parts with each member researching one part, or a group may decide to divide the work along the lines of sources, having one member look in encyclopedias, another in the reader's guide, and so on.

2. Students then go to the library to gather information with each member completing a questionnaire about the research he or she is doing. I use the same form as the one used in the previous lesson.

3. After returning to the room, each group compiles its information and develops its presentation.

4. Each group presents its information to the class.

Evaluation:

Students are evaluated on their individual work completed in the library (the Research Questionnaire) and on the work the group does. You may choose to use the Research Planner as part of a rubric that also includes the group's presentation. I usually add to the rubric a way to award points for the process the groups go through in order to get from the planning stage to the presentation stage.

Research Planner

Group's Topic: _____

In order to make the best use of your group's time in the library, you need to spend some time planning a strategy. You may decide to break the topic into parts with each member responsible for one part, or you may decide to divide all the possible sources among your group with each member being responsible for gathering information from one source.

After your group has made its decision, record your choices here.

Group Member	Responsibility

Lesson Four

Activity: Research Reports/Individual

Timeline: 3–4 days

Materials Needed: Instruction Sheet

Learning Objectives: Students will (1) research the origin of their names; (2) cite sources found in the library; and (3) cite sources of oral information.

Lesson Summary: Students will research the source and meaning of their own names and write a short paper on the information they found (using correct documentation methods for both written and oral sources).

The Activity:

This activity, begun when students were curious about a character's name, is one that I try to incorporate into my lessons at the beginning of the year, always tying it to the name of one of the characters in the literature we are reading at the time. I spend time explaining the idea of citing sources, showing students examples of the correct way to document both written and oral sources. We discuss the different ways to footnote, but for this exercise I ask that they use informal citations. I make sure they know how they will be graded for their work (both oral and written), and then they begin their search. Students tend to complain less about having to research if they are the topic of their investigations, and this simple activity allows them to practice for *real* research in a non-threatening way.

Lesson Outline:

1. After receiving and discussing the Instruction Sheet, students will use both the library and their own families to try to discover the meanings of their own names.

2. After gathering their information, students will write a short paper detailing their discoveries and using correct documentation methods for both the written and the oral sources of the information they gathered.

3. Students will give an oral presentation of their discoveries to the class and give the teacher their papers.

Evaluation:

Since this exercise is done at the beginning of the year when students are not yet fully comfortable with presenting to the class, I spend time preparing them for the actual presentation and detailing how they will be graded for it. We discuss the problems they may have and ways to work through those problems.

For example, some students want their finished paper with them during the presentation, and this can result in them merely reading the paper. Since this is not an exercise in reading, I suggest that if they feel more comfortable having something written to refer to that they use a notecard on which they have outlined what they want to say. This gives them the security of being able to refer to the card if they momentarily forget something, yet, at the same time, relieves them from the compulsion to read word-for-word from a paper. Allowing students to discuss what has bothered them in the past, and letting them help each other with suggestions, sets the tone for the type of presentations I prefer in my classroom—relaxed exchanges of information. However, there are times when I do grade presentations and this is one of them. For this, I usually use a rubric similar to the one below.

Item	Point Value	Points Earned	Total
Eye Contact: Looked around room	33		
Voice: Volume and rate appropriate	34		
Information: Required material	33		

You can see by the rubric that my focus during this exercise is to train students to care about the presentation style as much as the substance of the report. Since this report is about them, they tend to cover the information thoroughly.

I develop a similar rubric for the paper the students turn in. Keeping the focus on learning what types of information need citations and how to document their citations correctly, I weigh the rubric more heavily in those areas.

Instructions

Our names are used each day, by ourselves as well as by others, yet we seldom give them much thought. However, for the next few days you will be giving considerable thought to your name. By the end of this activity, you will have written a paper and given a presentation based on what you've learned about your name.

You will need to look for written information about your name and information that you can get by talking with your family. Most names have a historical meaning. Does yours? What is it? Parents often spend a lot of time and thought in selecting a name for their child. Why did your parents choose the name you have? If you were named after someone, what do you know about that person? Your task is to find out as much information about your name as you can in the time given and then to prepare that information for an oral presentation and a written paper. Both will be graded.

Lesson Five

Activity:	Research Reports/Groups
Timeline:	4–5 days
Materials Needed:	Library Project Forms
Learning Objectives:	Students will (1) divide into small groups; (2) research a topic dealing with revolutions; (3) make decisions based on their findings; and (4) present their decisions to the class.
Lesson Summary:	Students divide into small groups and then are given an Instruction Sheet that details the topic for their research. After researching their topic, each group makes decisions about revolution based on its findings and then presents its decision to the class.

The Activity:

I developed this activity as a way of presenting the viable concepts in *Animal Farm*, regardless of the Russian history upon which it was based. Truly not knowing what the students would discover in their research, nor anticipating what their decisions would be, I designed a task that required us to look at the results of revolutions in other times and places. The countries/times whose revolutions we investigated were: El Salvador, Cuba, China, France, the United States, Iran, South Africa, and Mexico.

I have since learned that this type of group research, requiring students to make decisions based on their findings, is a good way to look at other topics as well. For instance, a similar process could be used to investigate the effects of prejudice or poverty in various places and times. The success of the project would hinge on the decisions the students would be making, and I have found it best to ask them to accept or refute axioms dealing with the topic they are investigating.

Lesson Outline:

1. Divide students into groups and give each group a Library Project Form. Other than each group being assigned a different country to research, each Project Form has the same information.

2. The class discusses the project so that each student is clear about what is expected. Each group then plans its research (see Research Planner, Lesson Three).

3. Groups go to the library to research their countries.

4. Upon returning from the library, each group discusses its findings and reaches a conclusion about the axioms.

5. Groups present their conclusions to the class. I usually allow time at the end of the presentations for students to come to a classwide decision about the axioms.

Evaluation:

Giving a single group grade, based on the process rather than the outcome, works best with this project. If the groups work diligently on their research, base their decisions on their findings, and cover all the information necessary to explain their decisions in their presentation, they will have accomplished what the activity required. You could very easily make individual grades a part of this exercise by requiring students to keep individual Research Trackers or prepare individual written reports about either their findings or their process. Be sure that students understand at the beginning how they will be graded.

Animal Farm
Library Project

Country: _____

Group Members: _____

    The following are topics and questions you should consider before your group makes a decision on whether this country's revolution supports the statements below.

Government:

Prior to the revolution — What people were in control of the government? How were they selected? How were laws enacted? How were they enforced? Were all people represented equally? Was the government a democracy? A dictatorship? A totalitarian state?

After the revolution — What happened to those who had been in power? What people came into power as a result of the revolution? How were they selected? How were laws enacted/enforced? Were all people equally represented? What form of government developed?

Economics:

Prior to the revolution — What was the major industry or product? Was there a difference between the income levels/life styles of the ruling class and those who were not in political power? What type of interaction was there between socio-economic groups? What provisions were made for the basic needs of those unable to work?

After the revolution — Was there a change in the country's major industry or product? What happened to the socio-economic level of those who had been in power? Was there an increase in the wealth or lifestyle of those who came into power? Was there a leveling of wealth? Did it reverse? Stay the same? How were those unable to work treated?

Press:

Prior to the revolution — Was there a "free" press? What happened to those who were vocal opponents of the government? Were citizens able to meet freely and talk openly? How did most citizens receive information?

After the revolution — What happened to journalists who had been in favor of those who had been in power? Was there now a "free" press? Was there open opposition to those who came into power? How did most citizens receive information?

Other areas to investigate:

Propaganda — look at slogans, songs, flags, promises, goals, and so forth used by those in power both before and after the revolution.

Education — compare the educational level of those in power with the majority of the citizens both prior to and after the revolution.

Statements:

Absolute power corrupts absolutely.
All revolutions are doomed to fail.
Education and clear thinking of the masses can prevent absolute rule.

Bibliography

Adorjan, C. M. (1988). *WKID: Easy radio plays.* Niles, IL: A. Whitman.

Allport, G. W. (1979). *The nature of prejudice.* Reading, MA: Addison-Wesley.

Aresty, E. B. (1966). *The best behavior: The course of good manners—from antiquity to the present—as seen through courtesy and etiquette books.* New York: Cooper Square.

Arnow, J. (1995). *Teaching peace: How to raise children to live in harmony.* New York: Berkeley.

Axelrod, R. M. (1984). *The evolution of cooperation.* New York: Basic Books.

Barth, R. S. (1990). *Improving schools from within: Teachers, parents, and principals can make the difference.* San Francisco: Jossey-Bass.

Bissinger, K. (1990). *Leap into learning: Teaching curriculum through creative dramatics and dance.* Austin, TX: Nancy Renfro Studios.

Branscombe, A., Goswami, D., & Schwarz, J. (1992). *Students teaching, teachers learning.* Portsmouth, NH: Heinemann.

Brittain, W. L., & Lowenfeld, V. (1964). *Creative and mental growth.* New York: Macmillan.

Bruns, J. H. (1992). *They can but they don't: Helping students overcome work inhibition.* New York: Viking.

Calliope dances: A Renaissance revel. (1982). Los Angeles: Elektra/Asylum/Nonesuch.

Campbell, J. (1995). *Understanding John Dewey: Nature and cooperative intelligence.* Chicago: Open Court.

Characters from English literature. (1994). Walsenburg, CO: English Images.

Corridan, K. (1996, April). Reading, writing, and busy moms. *Redbook,* 153.

Davenport, D. (1992). Dismantling white/male supremacy. In C. M. Hurlbert & S. Totten (Eds.), *Social issues in the English classroom* (pp. 59–75). Urbana, IL: NCTE.

Dunbar, R. E. (1994). *How to debate.* New York: F. Watts.

Elements of art. (1979). Washington, DC: Gallaudet College, The School.

Farber, B. (1987). *Making people talk.* New York: Morrow.

Fiderer, A. (1995, October). Show me what you know. *Instructor.*

Gardner, H. (1993). *Multiple intelligences: The theory in practice.* New York: Basic Books.

Gaskill, A. R. (1990, Fall). What our public schools should be teaching. *Education.*

Graves, D. H. (1991). *Build a literate classroom.* Portsmouth, NH: Heinemann.

Graves, D. M. M. (1989). *Expecting the unexpected: Teaching myself and others to read and write.* Portsmouth, NH: Heinemann.

Gunzenhauser, M. (1996). *The square dance and contra dance handbook.* Jefferson, NC: McFarland.

Hayden, R. (1996). Training parents as reading facilitators. *Reading Teacher, 49,* 334–336.

Healy, J. M. (1986). *Is your bed still there when you close the door?: And other playful ponderings.* New York: Morrow.

Healy, J. M. (1990). *Endangered minds: Why our children don't think.* New York: Simon & Schuster.

Jaynes, J., & Wlodkowski, R. J. (1990). *Eager to learn: Helping children become motivated and love learning.* San Francisco: Jossey-Bass.

Johnson D. W., Johnson, R. T., & Holubeck, E. J.(1988). *Cooperation in the classroom.* Edina, MN: Interaction Book Co.

Kameenui, E. J. (1996, Winter). Shakespeare and beginning reading: The readiness is all. *Teaching Exceptional Children, 27* (2), 77–81.

Kaye, P. (1991). *Games for learning: Ten minutes a day to help your child do well in school.* New York: Farrar, Straus, Giroux.

Kennedy, D. (Ed.). (1986). *Community dances manual* (Vols. 1–7). Princeton, NJ: Princeton Book.

Kilpatrick, W. (1992). *Why Johnny can't tell right from wrong: Moral illiteracy and the case for character education.* New York: Simon & Schuster.

King, M. L. (1991). *Women of the Renaissance*. Chicago: University of Chicago Press.

Kraus, K. (1978). *Murder, mischief, and mayhem: A process for creative research papers*. Urbana, IL: NCTE.

Kronberg, R. (1993). *Clever folk: Tales of wisdom, wit, and wonder*. Englewood, CO: Libraries Unlimited.

Kyvig, D., & Marty, M. (1976). *Your family history: A handbook for research and writing*. Arlington Heights, IL: Harlan Davidson.

Leisner, T. (1980). *The official guide to country dance steps*. Secaucus, NJ: Chartwell Books.

Levin, D. E. (1994). *Teaching young children in violent times: Building a peaceable classroom*. Cambridge, MA: Educators for Social Responsibility.

Lewis, K. (1975, March). Putting the hidden curriculum of grading to work. *English Journal, 83*.

Lord, L. (1970). *Collage and construction in school: Preschool/junior high*. Worcester, MA: Davis Publications.

Lucas, E. (1991). *Peace on the playground: Nonviolent ways of problem-solving*. New York: F. Watts.

Markova, D. (1996). *The open mind: Discovering the six patterns of natural intelligence*. Berkeley, CA: Conari Press.

Martinet, J. (1996). *The art of mingling*. Arburn, CA: Audio Patterns.

McClatchy, J. D. (Ed.). (1988). *Poets on painter: Essays on the art of painting by twentieth-century poets*. Berkeley: University of California Press.

Millar, J. F. (1985). *Elizabethan country dances*. Williamsburg, VA: Thirteen Colonies Press.

Milord, S. (1994). *Tales alive! Ten multicultural folk tales with art, craft and creative experiences*. Charlotte, VT: Williamson.

Mischel, F. (1988). *How to write a letter*. New York: F. Watts.

Morris, N. C., & Kaplan, I. (1994). Middle school parents are good partners for reading. *Journal of Reading, 38*, 130–131

Morrison, J. E. (Ed.). (1975). *A choice selection of American country dances of the revolutionary era, 1775–1795.* New York: Country Dance and Song Society of America.

Murray, D. M. (1989). *Expecting the unexpected: Teaching myself—and others—to read and write.* Portsmouth, NH: Boynton/Cook/Heinemann.

Pavan, B. N. (1992). The benefits of nongraded schools. *Educational Leadership, 50,* 22–25.

Perkins, D. N. (1992). *Smart schools: From training memories to educating minds.* New York: Free Press.

Puckett, J. (1989). *Foxfire reconsidered: A twenty-year experiment in progressive education.* Urbana: University of Illinois Press.

Rakes, G. C., Rakes, T. A., & Smith, L. J. (1995). Using visuals to enhance secondary students' reading comprehension of expository texts. *Journal of Adolescent and Adult Literacy, 39,* 46–54.

Richards, J. C., & Gipe, J. P. (1993). Getting to know story characters: A strategy for young and at-risk readers. *Reading Teacher, 47,* 78–79.

Rieke, R. D. (1975). *Argumentation and the decision making process. New York:* Wiley.

Schick, L. (1991). *Heroic worlds: A history and guide to role-playing games.* Buffalo, NY: Prometheus Books.

School gripes. (1991, April/May). *Zillions,* 26.

Sculley, M. (1994, January). Family involvement. *Instructor,* 94.

Segal, T. (1992, March 30). Better schools, not just more school. *Business Week,* 93.

Seymour, D. (1992). *America's best classrooms: How award-winning teachers are shaping our children's future.* Princeton: Peterson's Guides.

Strickland, J., & Strickland, K. (1993). *Uncovering the curriculum: Whole language in secondary and postsecondary classrooms.* Portsmouth, NH: Boynton/Cook/Heinemann.

Sunn, R. S. (1993). *Bringing out the giftedness in your child: Nurturing every child's unique strengths, talents, and potential.* New York: J. Wiley.

Tannen, D. (1984). *Conversational style: Analyzing talk among friends.* Norwood, NJ: Ablex.

Tannen, D. (1986). *That's not what I meant!: How conversational style makes or breaks your relations with others.* New York: Morrow.

Tythacott, L. (1995). *Dance.* New York: Thomson Learning.

Unell, B. C. (1995). *Twenty teachable virtues: Practical ways to pass on lessons of virtue and character to your children.* New York: Perigree.

Wallace, B. (1995). *Poisoned apple: The bell curve crisis and how our schools create mediocrity and failure.* New York: St. Martin's Press.

Ward, W. L. (1957). *Playmaking with children from kindergarten through junior high school.* New York: Appleton-Century-Crofts.

Wigginton, E. (1985). *Sometimes a shining moment: the Foxfire experience.* Garden City, NY: Anchor Press/Doubleday.

Wigginton, E., (Ed.). (1991). *Foxfire: 25 years.* New York: Doubleday.

Wolf, A. (1990). *Something is going to happen: Poetry alive.* Asheville, NC: Iambic.

Wolff, S. (1974). *Games without words: Activities for thinking teachers and thinking children.* Springfield, IL: Thomas.

Wood, G. (1992). *Schools that work: America's most innovative public education programs.* New York: PLUME.

Zindel, P. (1992). *The pigman and me.* New York: HarperCollins.

Encourage Your Students to Think Outside the Box.

Subscribe to *Creative Kids,* "The National Voice for Kids."

Creative Kids is written for kids, by kids, and features original poetry, short stories, games, artwork, and much more. It's jam-packed with great ideas and fun commentary to inspire your students to think outside the box.

A favorite of teachers and kids for nearly 20 years, *Creative Kids* has recently undergone changes to reflect the tastes of the new millennium. While still appropriate for young readers, we're a bit edgier, funnier, and smarter . . . just like kids today. See why *Creative Kids* is the nation's largest magazine written for kids, by kids.

Let your students' voices be heard by submitting their very best work to *Creative Kids.* Anything that can be reproduced on a page can be considered for publication as long as it is suitable for readers ages 8–14.

The National Voice for Kids
CREATIVE KIDS
Volume 23   Number 3   Spring 2005

In This Issue:
• *Creative Kids* Gets a Brand-New Look
• Culinary Fairy Tale
• Amusement Park Musings
• And Much, Much, More!

Try *Creative Kids* for FREE!

Simply call us at (800) 998-2208 and we'll send you a trial issue of Creative Kids. After you receive your first trial issue, we'll bill you $19⁹⁵ for a year subscription. Your satisfaction is guaranteed. We're pretty confident that your students will like it, too.

One-Year Subscription: $19.95
Quarterly
Creative Kids
PO Box 8813
Waco, TX 76714-8813